Helmut Schuster and David Oxley are long-time collaborators and former work colleagues. It is their shared outlook that has bound them together as authors. They are optimistic futurists, advocates for next-generation talent, pioneers of new approaches to work, enthusiasts for new technology adoption, and crusaders against entrenched thinking.

As Drs Schuster and Oxley, they have set out to address several subjects that have been over-intellectualised, complicated, misdiagnosed, or outdated. With a whimsical eye and deep belief in humanity's strength to prevail against the absurdity of aspects of modern society, they are committed to presenting helpful business and leadership concepts for the next generation.

Dr Helmut Schuster is a dual Austrian/British citizen who lives in London, UK. He is the former Group HR Director of BP PLC. Helmut is currently Chairman of the Board of Ivoclar Vivadent AG, an active entrepreneur, investor, and frequent contributor to leadership and AFS Intercultural programs. Helmut was awarded his doctorate in Economics from the University of Vienna.

Dr David Oxley is a dual UK/US citizen based in Austin, Texas. David started his career as a management consultant before leading major people and corporate restructuring projects for BP PLC across Europe, the USA, India, and the Middle East. He worked closely with Reliance Industries in India, one of BP's partners, as they embarked on their big corporate restructuring. David was awarded his doctorate in Organisational Change at Cranfield University and his MBA from the University of Notre Dame.

To Sue, for everything.
To Elfriede, without whose encouragement I never would
have followed my passion.

Dr Helmut Schuster
and Dr David Oxley

A CAREER CAROL

A Tale of Professional Nightmares
and How to Navigate Them

AUST**I**N MACAULEY PUBLISHERS™

LONDON • CAMBRIDGE • NEW YORK • SHARJAH

A CIP catalogue record for this title is available from the British Library.

ISBN 9781035822461 (Paperback)
ISBN 9781035822478 (Hardback)
ISBN 9781035822492 (ePub e-book)
ISBN 9781035822485 (Audiobook)

www.austinmacauley.com

First Published 2023
Austin Macauley Publishers Ltd®
1 Canada Square
Canary Wharf
London
E14 5AA

Table of Contents

Disclaimer

The career crises summaries and suggestions in Part 2 are designed to provide accurate and authoritative information regarding the subject matter covered. The book is sold with the understanding that neither the authors nor the publisher is engaged in rendering legal, investment, accounting, medical, or other professional services. While the publisher and authors have used their best efforts in preparing this book, they make no representations or warranties with respect to the accuracy or completeness of the contents of this book and specifically disclaim any implied warranties of merchantability or fitness for a particular purpose. No warranty may be created or extended by sales representatives or written sales materials. The advice and strategies contained herein may not be suitable for your situation.

Preface

How do you approach the subject of careers, professions, and entrepreneurship in 2023? If you were asked what advice you would give to someone about to embark on their professional life, how would you go about it?

The post second world war order created a predictable and reliable platform for those living in Western-style economies: a stable society, a benign state, social mobility, accessible and affordable education, wealth generation, and security of work, income, and shelter. The advent of large multinational employers offered the implicit promise of lifelong employment and secures retirement.

On closer analysis, the popular depiction of 'jobs for life' was not exactly egalitarian or widely attainable. There were biases and glass ceilings baked in—a reflection of still immature attitudes to gender, sexual orientation, and race. The reality was more complicated. If one were attempting to give career advice to this generation, you might begin by saying, 'Start with being a white middle-class male'.

This said, there were some ingredients that seemed correlated to 'success'. Education, networks, communication, and interpersonal skills. Manufacturing serendipity. Understanding and harnessing the dark arts of leveraging connections in a largely analogue world.

The trouble with attempting to analyse and deliver advice about building successful careers on this level is that things have changed. And the pace of change, of what we now casually describe as 'disruptions', seems to be increasingly frequent. The past 20 years have marked a period of unprecedented technological advancement and, for some, huge wealth creation. Alongside this, has been significant progress on human rights, education, and a growing momentum on climate action. However, the end of this period has been impacted by three themes: first, the rise of populist national political movements; second, in March 2020, with the coronavirus pandemic; and third, the re-emergence of globally significant armed conflict.

Looking forward from 2023 and attempting to predict how these influences will shape the professional lives of today's generation of twenty- and thirty-somethings is difficult, if not foolish. They will be dynamic; they will be impacted by world events, and they will be shaped by societal attitudes and technology in complex ways. They will not be linear or analogue as they were 50 years ago. Beyond that, advice about maximising careers is in danger of repeating widely understood and clichéd subjects: get and maintain a good education, be more open-minded about entrepreneurship versus employment, change employers as frequently as fits your goals, hone your critical thinking skills, and balance fulfilment with financial security.

We, the authors of this book, have experienced our fair share of crises and disruptions throughout our professional lives. We have overcome these and, by many people's standards, been successful. So, is it reasonable to attempt to distil and share what we have learned to help the next generation? Experience is one of the most overrated and, at the same time, one of the least appreciated qualities. There is a lot of comfort in knowing that one has coped with so much adversity but that, in the long term, you can prevail and emerge stronger. Experience is very important, so long as it doesn't lead to stagnation and complacency. But we fully accept the context of our career journeys bridge between the contemporary analogue and digital career eras.

So, we have looked toward a deeper and less superficial level than that described above, with the intention of removing the contextual complexities. We have explored the intersection between major transitions during a normal human lifespan and how they manifest in a professional journey. Careers span some 40-plus years—roughly from age 20 to 60. During this time, people are also migrating to independence from parents, finding their moral roadmaps, understanding their values, understanding whether there is deeper fulfilment or purpose to life, and ultimately navigating into a post-career twilight. If we reframe the question of career advice to ask, 'What are the major existential crises an individual might be confronted with throughout their professional lives?' we get a potentially eternal question. Human beings, for millennia, have had to navigate different life phases. If we look at careers in this context, we believe we have a basis for bridging any contextual differences in generations. The life challenges we are referring to transcend the analogue-digital divide.

In this spirit, we wish to share our experience with the next generation. What wisdom we can muster in describing major existential career traps and how to navigate them. We believe that those in their twenties and early thirties have all that it takes to create a better world and progress in their chosen careers. But we also believe that this generation is facing much greater headwinds compared with those that preceded them. The complexities are greater. Complexities equal noise, distractions, and false signals. Achieving clarity of thought in an increasingly noisy world will be a far greater challenge for the readers of this book than it was for us.

We are conscious that hard-fought progress has been achieved in de-stigmatising mental health in recent years. According to the CDC, over 50% of us suffer mental illnesses or disorders in our lifetimes. Acknowledging this, as well as reducing the artificial barriers to providing helpful, and practical support, is very important. Writing a book about facing significant emotional trauma during your career clearly has mental health components to it.

We have, however, focused on sharing our pragmatic advice on how to navigate a long professional career successfully. Our stories and advice do not directly discuss the mental health challenges that may be implied.

About the book itself, it is a fable. We have both read our fair share of business books. Many, in our view, take a concept or finding and concoct ways to create 500 pages of sometimes dense text to justify publishing. We come from a distinctly different perspective. Our goal is to deliver our advice in an enjoyable, memorable, and succinct form. It is not by accident that we each listed at least two fables among our own top 10 business books of all time. They are fun to read, and the underlying messages are easy to see.

The story's main character, Shey—a conflicted, pre-college graduation member of Gen Z—is inspired by JD Salinger's Holden Caulfield but realised in our contemporary context. We use storytelling in Part 1 to draw out our themes for navigating successful careers, which we then analyse and translate into practical, pragmatic advice in Part 2. These are high-level, common-sense themes. However, that may only become obvious in retrospect.

This book is mainly targeted at a younger Western audience and those who work with them. However, it should be useful for anyone interested in their career, as most of the themes cross cultures and age boundaries.

Enjoy your time with Shey. We certainly have.

Part 1
A Career Carol

It Was the Night Before...
Graduation

… and all was still. Well, not exactly, still. The Bluetooth speaker in Shey Sinope's dormitory room played a low-mumbling song. If you strained your ears, you could just make out the lyrics… something low and mournful… depressing… bordering miserable. Shey had been doodling on his computer—one of his flights of fancy robot designs. However, he tried; he couldn't escape a dark mood. Tomorrow was his graduation day. This past four, well nearly five years, he'd gotten into a comfortable routine. Suddenly, he had to come to terms with the fact that his college days were over.

Shey viewed college much the same way he viewed most things in life; it was what he was doing right now. His parents had expected him to go, and he had passable grades at high school, so off to State University he went. The decisions and his path to this point had been pre-determined. He took the line of least resistance. Even at college, things had seemed pre-destined. His classes had been planned out and given to him at the beginning of each semester. He liked how the University's academic counsellors would guide him to the smoothest path for his degree credits, and his housing and meals were all part of the annual tuition package.

Where life was currently comfortable, routine, and easy, as much as he'd like to ignore it, he knew that tomorrow heralded a big upheaval for him. He had been in denial that this day would come. In fact, he'd gone to great lengths to distract himself. "Why worry about what happens after graduation when it is contingent on exams and credits that I haven't yet completed? Don't they say in sports that the secret of success is to focus on just the next game?" Tonight, however, it seemed the next game was graduation itself—the end of his predictable and comfortable college life.

Shey knew but hated that this might mean having to confront the persistent question he had been avoiding. "So, Shey, what do you plan to do after college?" Or the existentially phrased and much more intimidating sister question: "Shey, what do you want to do with your life?" He found these questions threatening. They were accusatory as if seeing through him to his core. He couldn't shake the feeling that even his most well-meaning relatives sensed the truth. Shey was a fraud. He had no idea what he was supposed to do. In those fleeting, painful moments when he tried to look within, he saw...nothing, just a void, a blank space.

Shey had developed a clever and highly effective tactic to sidestep these inquisitions. He found he could subvert an uncomfortable conversation by conjuring calculatedly obtuse responses, like, "I plan to maximise my opportunities while keeping my obligations to an absolute minimum!" Or "I want to be a pioneering inventor....in the field of grammar and abbreviation." And, of course, "I've always admired doctors, so if I can overcome my complete lack of aptitude in all the necessary fields of study, I'd certainly consider that." When he was in one of his darker moods, he might think, if not actually say, "Anything, as long as someone else just tells me where to go and what to do!"

"Shey, are you coming to this party tonight or not?" Ellen Elpis shouted through the door. "It's maybe your last chance to hang out with the crew."

Ellen was one of Shey's dorm neighbours. Even though she was one of the few people who might loosely be called his friend, Shey found her annoying, like a persistent rash that antibiotics could not seem to cure. Despite his best attempts, she seemed determined to try to get him to socialise and 'network'. She was always busy doing something, and while that was slightly irritating, it was her incessant optimism that was almost claustrophobic.

Shey got up and went to his room door. He opened it to find Ellen patiently standing outside. She wore one of her favourite sweatshirts with *One Young World Leadership Forum* on the lapel. Ellen had tried to get Shey to attend with

her, but he managed to avoid it. Honestly, Shey had told her, why do you want to waste a week of your life listening to a bunch of politicians and celebrities talk in clichés about world peace?

"No, I don't have time to go out tonight. I have some heavy-duty wrestling to do with my inner demons. My efforts this evening will free the world of at least two or three demons who might otherwise give some small kids a bad scare."

Ellen had heard variations of this answer before. "Well, I do think you've done your bit to exercise demons over the past few years. Maybe a break tonight will do you some good. Did you hear our commencement speaker is planning to come tonight? It would be a great opportunity to meet them before they give their big speech tomorrow."

"Well, now I'm definitely not coming! Honestly, what is the point of commencement speakers? All they do is give some generic speech about 'reaching for the stars' and 'believing in yourself'. It's all so gut-wrenchingly vomit-inducing." Shey sneered.

"Shey, don't be negative. I know that look. It's just a party, and, like most things in life, you can have fun if you want to."

"Commencement addresses, speeches, and the speakers themselves are so full of…. well, BS. Every address packages the same old forms of empty platitudes about making a mark on the world without one iota of substance. The speakers, most of the audience, and the faculty, all buy into a mass hallucination that the world is somehow navigable by a personal affirmation. That each of us is somehow able to bend the world to our wishes by being upbeat, bouncy, and motivated. The facts, quite clearly, point toward life being tough, filled with disappointments and heartbreak. How otherwise do you explain war, famine, disease, modern pop/rap fusion, social media trolls, and the puzzling popularity of the Mullet haircut?

"Then there's how most of these speakers achieved their own 'success.' They seem to have forgotten that their success was only an accidental by-product of huge swaths of capital looking to make a quick return on anything remotely connected with the latest faddish technology trend. Look at Theranos, Palm, Yahoo, Alta Vista, Netscape, and WeWork; are we really saying that the founders of these companies are people we want to take advice from? Perhaps on what not to do." Shey paused to see if he still had Ellen's attention, which, apparently, he did. "Don't even get me started on the politicians…. they use commencement speeches in much the same way as cult leaders seeking to exert mind control over their followers. It's all about 'do as I say and not as I do' and manipulative false indignation. Who can really take any of that seriously when they are at the same time making money from speaking to Wall Street firms, living double personal lives, and writing questionable murder mystery books with big-name novelists?

"Sports personalities, movie stars, and reality TV personalities are also laughably unqualified role models to take life advice from. How would any of them pass a moderate examination from Saint Peter on their net impact on humanity? After all, how does the genetic ability to throw a football, the reading of someone else's words with 'feeling', or the clever use of camera filters help advance our species? That only leaves missionaries and Red Cross leaders, and despite what many of our class might say, I know the vast majority really plan to be lawyers, stockbrokers, coders, entrepreneurs, or Instagram influencers. Except for that one guy who keeps talking about organic farming, but I have serious doubts his crop will have any measurable dietary use."

"Shey, I know you don't really believe that. Anyway, our commencement speaker doesn't fit into your cynical list of stereotypes. They have been successful on their own terms, created some amazing businesses, and, more recently, have been working to help solve some of our biggest societal challenges. I don't see how you could fail to learn something from them," said Ellen, immune to Shey's attempt to dampen her spirits.

"Oh, kill me now! Do you really believe they aren't just like all the others?" Shey paused and took a second for dramatic effect. "Ellen, you are too gullible. These big business names are all the same; they've sold their souls to the devils of consumerism and greed. One thing is for certain, you'll never catch me joining the ranks of the great corporate zombie masses! The thing I hate, above all else, that I detest with my very being are people who willingly accept a BS, meaningless corporate job just for a paycheque. I can't imagine how empty life would be if most of my time were spent in a prison constructed by a company that told me how I should behave and how I should look. All the while being forced to do busy work that no one really cared about and that I probably wouldn't even be very good at. All because some big entrepreneur thought they were somehow making lives better. What utter humbug!" He had nearly shouted the last few words.

"Do you feel a bit better?" said Ellen. "I do worry about you. Maybe you should have a quiet night."

As Ellen left the dorm, Shey felt his mood worsen. Normally, he felt better after he had shared wisdom. This evening, he felt depressed and empty. He closed his door. "Perhaps," he thought, "a cup of cocoa and browsing social media will help me feel better."

#

Ellen walked across the unusually deserted university quad toward the main reception room where the pre-graduation party would take place. On a late spring evening, it was getting dark early. There were heavy clouds in the sky. "Shey needs a friend, but he sure doesn't make it easy," she thought. Ellen's concern was heartfelt. She knew a good deal about feeling lost and alone. She had struggled to overcome crippling anxiety when she was younger.

Ellen decided to make a quick detour to the impressive faux Palace of Versailles fountain in the middle of the quad. The urban myth among students was that the fountain would grant wishes in certain special circumstances. She stood in front of the fountain, thought deeply for a moment, and bowed her head.

"I wish Shey finds his path. I wish he sees how great he can be if he could just look at the possibilities and not the obstacles."

Suddenly, Ellen felt the wind change and the sky darken. The campus streetlights flickered into existence. She jumped as a light bulb exploded behind her. There was a huge clap of thunder, and a bolt of pure energy struck the top of the statue in the middle of the fountain.

#

"Let this meeting of the commencement speakers of time and memoriam come to order," said Kurt Schmitt. Kurt had been elected as the chair of this most prestigious of all ghostly

societies in the late 1990s. "Order, order, now before we begin, does everyone have their sunscreen?" Kurt was famous for his skin care regiment.

"We have an urgent item to add to the agenda this evening. Let me see.... the annual baking competition dates, some updates on the proposal to do some extra haunting at the Crimson University's football coach's house, and what is this again.... member acceptance rules.... look, Steve, we've covered this before, we aren't banning anyone associated with Windows. Anyway, all of this will have to wait. We have received a message from the State University Faux-Palace of Versailles hotline. We referred this to our Carol committee, who recommended we launch a code red... tonight. I've passed you all a copy of their report. Can I take it you all agree?"

A loud chorus of "Yea" echoed as best it could over the clouds.

"The yea's have it. Jack, Ether, Sir Ant, Dr Frederick, and Dr Jon-Pierre, this looks like a job for your special talents. Are you up for the challenge?" said Kurt.

The five ghostly commencement society members stepped forward and nodded in unison.

Failure to Launch

"Phweeeeeeeeee!!" Shey was abruptly woken by an astonishingly loud whistle.

His room door burst open, and in marched a tuba, trumpet, and drum...along with their owners. The band launched into *Get Up Offa That Thing*. A few seconds later, four acrobats tumbled into sight and shouted, "Give me a J.... give me an A......give me a C.... give me a K.... that's right.... iiiiiitttt's JACK ... and he is back!"

"Let's Go.... Let's Go...RISE and SHINE.... it's time for the going to get tough young man!" shouted Jack Lightning. He was dressed in his customary 1960s grey suit and trilby hat, surrounded by an unmistakable luminescence.

"Wait a minute. Who are you, and how did you get into my room?" Shey was still trying to make sense of the situation. "I shouldn't have had that cup of cocoa...the milk smelled off."

"Young man, I am the first of four visitations that the society of ghostly commencement speakers will bestow on you tonight. We've taken a special interest in you and your cynical, disrespectful thoughts on our collective virtue. That, and someone with no reason to care about you, has made a very touching appeal. You are going to receive the greatest gift of all possible gifts...the chance to be confronted with choices and consequences you haven't yet made. The chance

28

to understand where they may lead and whether they are what you thought they were. In other words, it's your lucky night.... you're going to be scared out of your skin!" Jack boomed. "Like I always say, it's going to be déjà vu all over again...multiplied by four.

"I am the ghost of failed beginnings. It's the first quarter, and we are down by three touchdowns. It's time to start our comeback. Blocking and tackling will at best stop the other team from scoring, but is that all you want? To stand still...go nowhere? It's time to hold the mirror up and see who reflects

back!" Jack was fond of his aphorisms. "You have doubt Shey Sinope, doubt and fear. You run from your doubt. That leads, well, to failure, failure to learn, failure to evolve, to grow. Instead, what you need is to attack your doubt. Overload the line of scrimmage! Overpower it. Crush it. Doubt moves through uncertainty and becomes an opportunity, a story yet to be written. Your job is to ride BELIEF to GLORIOUS

VICTORY!" Jack had missed his touchline motivational pep talks, and boy, did this kid deserve one. "Three visitations will follow. Each will show you a possible future. Each will allow you to see where doubt, passiveness, denial, and moral erosion may lead you. Each will provide you with the opportunity to live these existential crises and reflect on how you could avoid them. I warn you now, these will not be comfortable or pleasant lessons. Each of my colleagues will expose themselves to you in due time. We'll see afterwards whether you still believe commencement speakers deal only in light entertainment and superficiality. Get ready for a HELL of a ride!"

Shey, mesmerised by Jack, shook his head to straighten his thoughts. Something deeply unsettling was happening. Could he escape? He looked out the window. That seemed a bit dramatic and possibly painful.

He thought, *well, if this is a dream, how would I normally shake it off?* He started to blink; he heard this helped wake you from a nightmare. It was as he was making some strange facial contortions that two huge football players rushed into the room and poured the contents of a 20-gallon cooler on his head.

#

Shey opened his eyes, realised he was magically dry, wearing jeans and an old college sweatshirt, and standing in someone's living room. He stood next to a beaten-up sofa. A second ago, he was soaked with an iced sports drink, talking to someone who claimed to be a ghost. Now he felt he'd been awoken from a dream, but he wasn't in the comfort and safety of his bedroom. He was in an unfamiliar house. Had he been asleep on this sofa? What was he doing in this strange house? How did he get here?

Shey surveyed the room. There was a TV with a game console. Someone had been playing *Robot Wars: Extreme Destruction*. There were empty pizza boxes. The room had not been cleaned or even tidied for a few weeks. As he walked across the living room, he caught a glimpse of himself in a mirror. "What the heck! That can't be me. The person in the mirror must be ten years older than me and... wait... a mullet haircut... that's just wrong!"

"YOU KNOW WHAT CARPE DIEM MEANS!?" shouted Jack, making Shey jump. "It means something about fish of the day, but that's not important right now. I'm going to show you what happens if you remain a prisoner of doubt. I have transported you, using my mystical ghostly powers, to a decade after college graduation. This is what awaits you if you fail to launch into the rest of your life. You have allowed yourself to drift. Beyond a point in life, friends and family start to see passengers as a burden. So, as I like to say, while you can observe a lot by watching, it will help you more if you live this day and find out what it really feels like. Enjoy!" And with that, Jack, a wide grin on his face, was hoisted on the shoulders of some familiar-looking football players, who then ran out of the house through one of the walls.

Shey spent the next hour in a disorientating search of the house. "This is a hell of a dream," he thought. "It's like an escape room mixed with an elaborate practical joke."

He seemed to be in a low-cost rental in a neighbourhood not far from his college. He had about $10 in loose change to his name, no credit cards, an expired driver's license, and a backpack with some unwashed clothes.

The only clues he found about the other residents of the house were strategically placed post-it notes containing less than inspiring messages. Above the stacked sink was "Shey, CLEAN THE DISHES." In the fridge, "Shey, HANDS OFF OUR FOOD." In the bathroom, "Shey, DON'T LEAVE A MESS." By the back door, "Shey, TRASHCANS ARE NOT TOYS!"

It seemed Shey wasn't in the running for housemate of the year. Moreover, he didn't like the ample evidence pointing to him being the resident house slacker. Did it follow that everyone else had gone to work? His pocket began ringing. He found a phone and answered.

"Shey, it's your mother. We'll be there to pick you up around three o'clock."

"Mum, I'm having the strangest dream. I may be running a fever. Can you call the campus police and have them check on me?"

"You're not making any sense, Shey. I know it's been a tough time for you—your roommates kicking you out—but you can't blame them. You haven't done your bit to pay any of the bills," said Shey's Mum.

"Wait, so I was living here? And they're kicking me out!? What exactly have I been up to these past few years?" Shey started to ask the right questions.

"Well, that's a first. Typically, you're so defensive when it comes to talking about the choices you've made and where they have led you. You know Dad and I will always support you, but even we have struggled with some of your stranger recent ventures. Honestly, you must have been the most overqualified ice cream van driver ever, although I'm still mad at them for the whole firing business. How *Mr Whippit Good* expected you to sell anything during the coldest winter on record, I'll never know."

"I'm an ice cream van driver?" Shey was disappointed.

"Well, you were. Right now, I think you are... what is your favourite phrase... maximising your opportunities while keeping your obligations to an absolute minimum?"

"Mum, you know I used to say that sarcastically. I didn't really mean it. It was just a way... a way to buy some time. I always assumed ...well, that something meaningful would emerge for me. What did I do after college?"

"I think he might have amnesia," the phone was muffled, and presumably, Mum was explaining to Dad where the conversation was going. "Let's stop and pick up some soup for him." To Shey, "Well, you did have those interviews right after college for some big companies, but you always seemed so pessimistic and negative. I'm not that surprised that they never came to anything. Then there was the backpacking around Asia, which ended early with you complaining it was hot and crowded. We were both pleased when you went back to school to do your masters."

"I have a master's degree!" Shey finally clung to some good news.

"Well, no, you did one semester and said it was a waste of time. If I recall, you said you could learn more on the internet for free, and you thought you'd developed a fatal allergic reaction to PowerPoint. You did also say that one time that you thought… perhaps… you were just avoiding something. It's a shame you haven't figured out what that was."

"So, to recap, I have basically done nothing these past ten years? God, what a loser I must be." Shey genuinely assumed that after college, he would find something meaningful. His life up until graduation had felt like he'd been swept along on a tide of others' plans and arrangements. Why shouldn't life after college have been the same?

"Well, you have accumulated some student loans, presumably figured out a few things you don't want to do, and of course, learned a valuable lesson about seasonality in the frozen dessert business." Mum could always be counted on to sum things up and make even the most depressing news sound mildly positive. "We'll see you at 3 o'clock, son. Maybe take a nap and see if that helps you feel better. Love you, bye."

Shey stood still for a minute with the phone silently pressed to his ear. "I don't accept this is anything more than a bad dream." But he had a sense of the lesson embedded in it.

He also knew he was once again attempting to avoid confronting an uncomfortable truth. He was anxious about where his life might go after college. While it was true that he lacked Ellen's apparent certainty on what to do next, he was also baffled about how to decide. He understood he was waiting for something, or someone, to show him a path. What if they never showed up?

The rest of Shey's day was no less painful than the phone call with his mum. He really was couch surfing, and it seems he had even failed at that. When most of his contemporaries would be thinking about reversing the polarity in the parent-child equation, his parents were coming to take him home, to rescue him. He was living a life without possessions, maybe even religion too. If he could have claimed some conviction about dropping off the grid, maybe it would have been better. He could then claim a cloak of some principled conviction. However, what seemed to sum up this existence was emptiness. He was experiencing a day that had no real meaning, no purpose, no objective, and no goals. It was *Groundhog Day*, but presumably, in his case, the date did change.

As he looked out of the window of Dad's old station wagon at the streetlights that passed by, he thought, *well, let's just make a pact right now, Shey Sinope. Let's just agree if or when we wake up from whatever this is, we never find ourselves back here again.* Shey closed his eyes.

#

"Well, laddie, did you leave it all on the field today?"

Shey was magically back in his dorm room with the luminous Jack Lightning standing imposingly in his doorway.

"I hated every minute of that…dream. And it wasn't fair, Mr. Lightning, not fair at all. You see, for that to ever happen, many people would have failed me. The college careers office, for one. Those guys get paid to make sure we all get jobs. Plus, what happened to my so-called friends? They obviously didn't try very hard to help me," Shey was relieved at being back in his room. He was starting to feel some of his old indignation and entitlement returning.

"The bed won't make itself; the resume won't write itself; the contact won't know you're alive unless you DO SOMETHING NOW!" Jack shouted, the irritation at Shey's persistent avoidance showing. "Mark these words Shey Sinope; take OWNERSHIP of your own future….no one else will. Take OWNERSHIP and then ACT; don't procrastinate. And, don't BLAME anyone else when things go wrong. It's an opportunity ALWAYS for you to ask how you could have avoided, navigated, and rebounded stronger. Hear these words and know them well. You have been warned; your fate is in your hands."

But how?" whispered Shey sheepishly.

"Phweeeeeeeeeee!!! By Jiminy, that's the most sensible thing you've said this evening!" Jack looked at his whistle and smiled fondly. "Yes, HOW? Well, that is just like I always say…. how do you get to Carnegie Hall? Buy a violin, of course!" And with that, Jack Lightning was gone.

Beware of Gilded Cages

Shey sat propped up in his bed in stunned silence. "Did that just happen?" He thought. "I've had some crazy dreams before, but that felt different. Almost real. And normally, I only remember snippets of my dreams. I remember *every* aspect of that one!"

"Mrrrrrrrrrawr…. meow…. mew", a tabby cat walked across Shey's open windowsill. "Mrrrrrrrrrawr…. meow…. screech," a second later, a nearly identical tabby cat repeated the same walk but wobbled and fell.

"Rats, I told props that wouldn't work," he heard someone just out of sight say.

Shey's phone pinged. He pulled himself away from the window and picked up his phone. He could see an old-school SMS was being typed from a number in California.

…wake up, Shey…
…the gilded cage is closer than you think…
…act now, or you may become a prisoner forever…
…look out your window…

"Ohoo," escaped Shey's lips. He had a very bad feeling about this. He could hear the screaming of a motorbike approaching. It sounded like there were several police cars in chase. He ran to his second-story window and peeked out. He could see an impressive figure falling off a motorbike.

"OK, let's go again, everyone!" Shouted a frustrated voice.

Shey watched in fascination as everything seemed to reset. A second later, the motorbike sped around the corner and screeched to a dramatic halt under his window. The rider jumped off, and a second, identical-looking figure took their place.

"Shey, no time to explain. You must come with me right now!" shouted the new figure, a microphone was suspended above their head.

"Arr…but why?" Shey shouted down.

"OK…that's not right. LINE…what's his line?" The bike rider barked. Someone in the shadows said, "Am I in trouble? What's going on? Are you here to save me?"

"Shey, deep breaths, you can do this. OK, let's go again."

Shey said nothing. He was too stunned. He counted at least six cameras, a food truck, and a few dozen people running around in the background.

"HEY! Shey, Focus! We don't have much time. I am Ether...well, technically, a ghost actor playing Ether, I am here to ask you an important question. One that could change your life. I am the ghost of gilded cages. The second visitation prognostication promised by the society of ghostly commencement speakers," she paused. "You may be sleepwalking toward a terrible fate. I am here to show you what may happen if you don't wake up.... not from this dream, I meant from the bigger danger. You know what, let me just show you!" One of the enormous theatrical spotlights exploded, and hot filament fountained down all around them.

Someone shouted: "And SCENE!"

#

Shey opened his eyes. He was surrounded by a beige, 1980s-style work cubicle. There was a grey desk with a vintage desktop computer sitting centrally. He sat in an uncomfortable, grey, semi-recliner chair. There were piles of papers in a tray marked 'in'. He felt claustrophobic almost immediately.

"Morning Shey, what's the word on the street?" Shey saw he held a coffee mug declaring 'Wes Winker, The Boss' in big, bold letters. "Mm-hmm ... you know, you said you needed some overtime hours? Why don't you come in tomorrow, Saturday, and Sunday as well? I need some help validating data reports. As you know, things are tight, so no paid overtime as such, but I can assure you, it will help when it comes to bonus time," Winker paused to slurp noisily from his mug of coffee. "So, if you could do that, that would be grrrreat!" Winker feigned someone else beckoning him and moved down row after row of identical beige office cubicles.

Well, he's a piece of work, Shey thought. He stood up to take a quick survey. The whole office was muted and crowded. He had heard stories of how evil office designers were in the 80s and 90s; it seemed like a giant half-size maze under a sky of strip lighting. "As dreams go, though, this doesn't seem so bad. It seems like I have a job. And, assuming Winker is the manager, he's leaning on me, so that's a good sign. He may be kind of creepy, but I'm at least glad this isn't another escape room." Suddenly he heard the noise of some pulleys and a zip line. He looked up.

Ether was suspended from the ceiling. She was wearing a green harness that seemed to be jammed. "Geez guys, this was fine in rehearsal...hold on…. I think I've got it," she thumped on the side of her harness and fell straight to the ground, just missing Shey.

She picked herself up. "Ouch. Well, the show must go on, right? Where were we…ok…Shey." She paused to remember her line and change her facial expression. She looked stern, grave, and ghostly, "All that glitters is not gold. Can you be trapped in a room without walls? Shey, today you get to experience how your life might be if many of the things you think you desire actually come to pass. Be careful what you wish for." The harness sprung violently back to life, and she whizzed back into the ceiling.

With only the murmur of white noise that followed, Shey took stock. He saw a monochrome spreadsheet staring at him. He saw rows and rows of numbers, each with a little comment box. The comment box simply said 'true' or 'false.' While he speculated whether that was essentially his job, he heard a rap on the side of his cubicle.

"Hey, buddy, I picked up your mail. It looks like there are some more final reminders in there. Plus, the last copy of your *PRACTICAL ROBOTICS* magazine subscription. Kills me you had to give that up. Did you get Winker to give you some overtime hours?" asked Shey's cubicle neighbour. His name tent read Joe Goliath.

"Well, seems like I got the overtime but not any pay," Shey replied.

"Isn't that just typical? Honestly, it sucks here. If the job market weren't so bad, I'd be out of here in a heartbeat. Hey, did you hear that Gastric Tech across the street flushed half their people? Very unrighteous," Joe whispered, "I hear we may be next."

"Yeah, maybe, but surely, we are much better off than some people. You know, like those parasite graduate dropout couch surfer losers?" Shey thought, however this might seem, it must be better than that last 'dream'.

"Really? Sometimes it seems like we have gone backwards, not forwards. If I was unemployed on a couch somewhere, I'd have nothing…sure. But right now, I might have less than nothing; I owe the bank a huge mortgage; I have an auto loan on a more expensive car than I can really afford; I'm behind on my credit card payments, and I still have an obscene student loan. And everything is getting more expensive, utility bills, groceries, while our pay has been flat this past two years. It seems as fast as I try to run, my bills run faster." Joe looked like he had the weight of the world on his shoulders.

"But maybe I'm doing ok. On a relative basis, at least. Luxury problems and all that?"

"You're joking, right?" Joe replied. "You have all my troubles, plus you absolutely hate your job. Sure, I think it sucks here, but you, well, what did you say? You always promised yourself you'd never get caught in a BS job? Just yesterday, you said you dreaded every new day because it would likely be the worst of your life. That's some crazy dark stuff!"

"I was afraid you might say something like that." Shey thought he understood where Ether had left him. Stuck in a horrible job and trapped by obligations, bills, and bad consequences if he didn't just stick it out. "Joe, tell me, what do you think we do here? How do you explain what this company does?"

"Well, as you know, I have a theory on this. The public face of this place is that we provide the software that the major players use to correct spelling and grammar in their word-processing apps. Hence the name Spellman Enterprises. But I think that's just a cover. The only explanation that makes sense is that this is some sort of government experiment in psychological warfare. Like virtual waterboarding, despicably designed to crush human souls." Joe was apparently an urban philosopher with conspiracy theory leanings.

There was some commotion in the reception area next to the elevators. A PA system bled some feedback before booming way too loudly: "EVERYONE, CAN I HAVE YOUR ATTENTION." It was Winker. "I have an important announcement for you all. Can you gather round?" The cubicle occupants slowly emerged from their hiding places and shuffled rather sadly over to where Winker was standing. Someone had tied some balloons to the PA system speaker, and there was a generic banner hastily taped to the ceiling. It read, "Congratulations on 25 years of loyal service _____" No one had thought to fill in a name.

Shey joined the crowd. He couldn't help but notice everyone was dressed similarly. Everyone seemed to have the same expression on their faces, one of thinly veiled boredom. He thought of worker bees, drones. He was just like everyone else. All individuality eliminated.

"Here at Spellman, we love our employees. While it is important that I emphasise we are a team, we are all equal in our mission to eradicate spelling and grammar errors; we hope you will join us in saying a quick thank you to Alfred Swing. Today marks Alfred's 25th year with us if you include the acquisitions and restructurings. Well done, Alfred! Please come forward; we have a $15 voucher for the *Olive Garden* here so you can go out tonight and celebrate. Alfred? Where are you?" Winker looked mildly irritated.

Joe turned to Shey and whispered, "Dumbasses haven't realised Alfred is on vacation this week. I don't think Winker even knows what he looks like. Hey, I have an idea." Joe suddenly marched forward and shook Winker's hand. He grabbed the voucher and then returned to the anonymity of the crowd.

"OK. Well alrighty, there we go," said Winker. "We have half a dozen cupcakes up here should any of you want a snack. Now back to work everyone!"

Shey couldn't take this anymore. He ran to the elevators and rushed out of the building. He didn't know where he was going; he just couldn't stand to be in that office a second longer. Was it just yesterday that he had been talking about BS jobs and corporate prisons? Well, at the time, he was only saying it to undermine Ellen and shoot down the whole 'entrepreneurs create amazing places to work' theme. Now, having lived this…dream…hallucination. Well, it was far worse than he could have imagined. Joe was right; this was worse than couch surfing. In this reality, life has no meaning, no purpose, but it also seems to have no means of escape. In the couch surfing dream, you could still imagine an escape. Here, well, the future was eclipsed, erased almost, by the need to run on a pointless hamster treadmill.

"I can accept struggle for a purpose," he thought. "I can see the point of suffering for an ideal. But how could I navigate my way into a situation where I end up struggling and suffering for nothing. Could I really become so terribly confused that I might consciously and willingly make decisions that would lead me here?"

He stood feeling very lost on the deserted sidewalk outside the office. He looked to the horizon. The sun seemed to be setting like someone was using a dimmer switch on a giant spotlight. The darkness slowly gathered pace…it rushed toward him. He realised at the last minute that he was being faded to black.

#

A second after the darkness surrounded him, he heard, "Cue spotlight… and… ACTION!" Ether stood outside Shey's dormitory building, silhouetted in simulated moonlight. It was raining. Well, there was a guy spraying water over them from a fire engine.

"Unfortunately, no one can be told what the gilded cage is. You must see and experience it for yourself. In this reality, choice seems like an illusion, a suffocating illusion," Ether said.

"But I don't understand how that could ever happen. I absolutely don't want to work for a bad company doing a BS job. I already know this." Shey was desperate to avoid this future.

"Shey, life is cumulative. No single decision or choice leads to the gilded cage. You step down the path slowly, one small but incremental step at a time. Recognise first that you know you like to have choices made for you. You have admitted this, even said you prefer it. If you continue to live an unconscious, purposeless existence, you risk this destination. The gilded cage is an outcome achieved by going with the flow. By measuring your success with artificial materialistic measures; by unquestionably following the herd; by believing happiness can be achieved by comparison to others. BE WARNED, the gilded cage awaits you if you follow this path. BE CAREFUL, Shey, because if you find yourself in the gilded cage, it is like quicksand. It will try to pull you deeper and deeper."

"And that's a wrap, people!" Someone shouted to muted cheers.

The crowded production set evaporated with a loud clapperboard snap.

The Fallacy of Blind Faith

It took Shey a few moments to gather himself. The production crew seemed to have vanished. The streets were still glistening with the after-effects of the fake rain. He turned toward his dormitory lobby. As he did, a beautiful classic Rolls Royce purred to a halt in one of the parking spots. The driver's door opened, and a distinguished-looking man stepped out of the car. He was a tall, thin man, maybe in his 70s, with a thick swathe of slicked-back grey hair, a monocle, and a debonair moustache. He wore an expensive three-piece suit, complete with a pocket watch.

"Ahh...excuse the interruption, dear boy. I am Sir Anthony Bark. Most people call me Sir Ant. Pleased to meet you."

"Are you lost, professor? You know the faculty accommodation is over on the west side of campus? Do you need directions?" said Shey.

"Oh, yes...no...no...hahaha... I may have given you the wrong impression. No, you see, I am quite in the right place and, I think, time, yes, let me see," he took out his pocket watch and flipped the lid. "Yes, perfect. Right place, right time. And you must be Master Shey Sinope. Is that correct?"

Shey knew instantly he was in trouble. However, he felt a certain anticipation, maybe excitement. These visitations were coming thick and fast. Presumably, this gentleman, Sir Ant, was another ghost.

"Sir Anthony, are you a ghost?"

"Indubitably. A spirit. An apparition, a spook, a phantom. Yes, indeed. I am the third visitation promised to you tonight. I am the ghost of blind faith. Let me see... yes... Boooo... Whoo-oo... and...OoOoOoOoh..." Sir Ant didn't seem to have mastered his spooky haunting skills. "Can we dispense with the whole 'scary ghost' business? It is quite tiresome. I would prefer it if we could take a ride in the Rolls. I can show you what you need to see."

"Ok. I gather you have a job to do, and I appreciate you being pleasant," Shey said.

"Well, where would my manners be otherwise? Please take a seat, young Shey. Fasten your seatbelt. Would you care for a lemon drop? No? They are my favourite."

Shey was warming to this ghost. The doors on the car closed automatically, and the engine whined and then roared frighteningly.

I wonder if ghost cars have safety inspections? Shey thought. *Hopefully, it doesn't blow up.* As he completed his thought, the car disappeared from the parking lot with a modest nuclear explosion.

"This isn't a normal car, is it, Sir Ant?" Shey prided himself on his deductive capabilities.

"Good spot. No, it's an invention of my own making. One of several I have dabbled with over the years. Between inventing the odd useful gadget and starting a few industries, I've always tried to keep myself busy. Idle hands and all that," replied Sir Ant. "It's a multi-dimensional tin opener, really. No big deal. Theoretically, I can make these journeys without the Rolls, but if you must travel, I've always believed it should be in a certain style."

Shey thought in different circumstances, he would have loved to talk to Sir Ant about robotics. However, Sir Ant was clearly busy, and Shey didn't want to distract him from driving a nuclear-powered vehicle. He could see very little out of the car windows. The Rolls seemed to be travelling in a void. In the far distance, Shey could just make out a small dot of light. "Sir Ant, is that where we are going?"

"Absolutely, that is our destination. Now hold on, the landings are always the darndestly difficult and uncomfortable to pull off." Sir Ant hit a few colourful buttons on his dashboard, played with the steering wheel, and then honked the horn. There was a blinding light, and they materialised on a cart path next to a textile factory in Nottingham, England. The factory was surrounded by a rowdy group of men and women. "Welcome to northern England, c.1812. Let me introduce you."

As they emerged from the Rolls, a man who looked like the mob's leader launched a Molotov cocktail through the factory window. The crowd cheered. Sir Ant strolled up to the man.

"Mr Ludd, Mr Ludd…. may I introduce you to my new friend Master Shey Sinope," Sir Ant ushered Shey forward. "I believe he can learn a great deal from you, Mr. Ludd. Would you mind sharing some thoughts with him?"

Mr Ludd did a double take. Given the surrounding mayhem, his attention seemed understandably torn. "Well, it's not that complicated really," began Mr Ludd, "these 'ere factory owners are oppressing the working man. Through their shameless pursuit of profits, they have caused enormous social suffering. We are here to teach them a lesson. Nothing changes around here unless we, the workers, agree." Mr Ludd's face began to turn red with anger.

"Well, indeed, no doubting your conviction and commitment to the cause, Mr Ludd," said Sir Ant. He then turned to Shey and said, "My gift to you, Master Shey, this most providential night…is to walk in Mr Ludd's shoes, well, more accurately, those of some of his decedents. Let you make up your mind whether he is right." They both turned around to see a group of red-coated soldiers charging toward them. "Oi," they shouted. "Ludd, you bleedin' troublemaker." Shey noticed they were rather indiscriminate in using their muskets to beat all in their path as they made a beeline for him and Mr Ludd. He turned to see Sir Ant had returned to the Rolls.

Suddenly, he felt a huge thump on his head, and the lights went out.

Shey regained consciousness while sitting in front of a huge bank of wires and sockets. The bank seemed to stretch 50 feet in both directions. He was one of around 20 people facing the machine while wearing a one-ear headset. He heard his neighbour say, "Hello, this is the operator, which number… please hold… connecting."

"Mr Ludd," said a voice behind him. "Do you need to take a break? Please go ahead for 15 minutes. Off you go," and directed Shey, who, as Sir Ant had promised, was walking in a Mr Ludd's shoes. Shey found his way to a small break room at the end of the bustling switching apparatus. He saw three people waiting expectantly as he approached.

"Mr Ludd, tell us more about what you think we should do. The phone company seems intent on moving ahead with the job cuts. Do you think we can really stop them? I hear the switching centre in San Francisco has already closed. Apparently, people can now call direct." One of the telephonists asked.

Shey wasn't sure how to respond. It was reasonably commonplace, he thought, for companies to reorganise and lay people off. Why should these people think they can stop the wheels of commerce? "Well, what did I tell you before?" he responded.

"You said we should go on strike—a mass walkout. Bring management to their knees. Then, if that failed, well, we should consider escalating, which sounded ominous, but you didn't really say what you meant. What should we do? I have a family to support and bills to pay. This job is all that's between me and living on the street."

As Shey was about to respond, a group of security guards emerged from behind a filing cabinet. "We've got you, Ludd, in mid-conspiracy again. You're coming with us."

Shey was set upon by the enthusiastic guards who were intent on pre-empting any attempt to resist. He felt another bonk on his head, and again the lights went out.

#

Shey opened his eyes and saw a computer screen on a small desk in a modern open-plan office. His head was thumping. Those guards clearly had it in for him. He looked around to see if anyone else was about to try to attack him. Mercifully the office seemed quiet.

As he surveyed his surroundings, he saw framed magazine covers hung on the walls. There was a bright neon sign hanging at one end declaring 'TRUTH IS WORTH WRITING FOR.' He guessed that he was in the office of a magazine publisher. By the looks of his open laptop, he was working on a story. He read the first few lines, "Let's keep news human, and let's keep the news alive! The time has come to say enough is enough! Journalists bring a level of creativity and ethical judgment that will never be replicated by the emerging machine-generated content. Perhaps many of our readers are unaware that an increasing percentage of your newspapers, news websites, and magazines are written not by people but by AI algorithms. If we don't act now, then the profession of journalism as we know it will be quietly but brutally eradicated. Beyond the tragic personal consequences to journalists, think of the terrible risks of allowing our society to have opinion shaped by a series of 'what/if' equations."

"Ludd…. Hey, aren't you coming to the demonstration? I thought you were one of the most vocal organisers?" A figure wearing a corduroy suit and beret appeared next to Shey's desk. "Come on; it's about to start."

Shey followed via the elevator and out into the street below. There was a gaggle of people forming a circle. Each was holding a placard with a variety of slogans on the theme of journalism being an endangered species. Someone handed Shey a placard, and a chant began to gather voice: "TRUTH OVER PROFITS, ETHICS BEFORE CLICKS," and

"TECHNOPHOBIA NOT HIPPOPOTOMONSTROSES - QUIPPEDALIOPHOBIA." A small crowd grew around the protesters. A second later, a black police SWAT van skidded to a halt beside them. An intimidating group of riot police jumped out. Several made a beeline for Shey who immediately crouched and protected his head.

Shey opened his eyes. He was sitting in the Rolls again. Sir Ant sat next to him. "So, what did you learn, young Shey? Was Mr Ludd accurate in his convictions? More importantly, what lessons can we take from this quick trip through the recent graveyard of human professions?"

"Well, the Ludds have resilient skulls and a definite affection for fighting seemingly lost causes!" Shey instinctively checked his head for signs of trauma. "If the point here is about how society protects those with power and influence, I think I knew that. The workers do tend to get the poor end of capitalist business cycles. I don't know I like it. But is the lesson that resistance is futile? These worker revolts always end the same way... painfully for the workers."

"Ummmm...yes... well...no... no. You have observed the rearguard battles; most I suspect you already knew. My question is whether you have considered the personal implication. The choice, if you will, that these societal forces imply for the discerning and informed individual. Let me first ask you this. Do you think Mr Ludd's descendants end with journalism or whether their fate is an infinite struggle?"

"It does seem like the pace of technological disruption is coming faster and faster nowadays. My cousin just lost his job at the travel agency he was working in. People just book online nowadays. I also heard that they even have software now that does the hiring process for companies. So, I suppose the answer is these professional extinctions will continue and maybe accelerate?" replied Shey.

"Agreed. So, how should an individual manage this? It is a 'known-known,' after all. As a scientist, I find it tiresome when people are surprised by the laws of nature. The Darwinian Theory applied to professions. This is the lesson of blind faith. You have a choice, young Shey. You can choose to be a small boat on the sea of technological disruption. At the mercy of its frightening power. If you place your faith in a single company, profession, or set of skills, you will inevitably fall foul of these bigger forces. However, alternatively, you can choose to be informed, forewarned, and change the metaphor to being a skilled surfer riding the successive waves." Sir Ant paused and turned to meet Shey's gaze directly. "Master Shey, if you live the rest of your life in the blind faith that employers, society, or other people will protect you from obsolescence, you, like the Ludds, will likely feel persecuted and oppressed. Choose instead to be proactive, predictive, and plan accordingly. IF YOU DON'T REINVENT YOURSELF EVERY 10 YEARS, YOU WILL LIKELY BECOME, AT BEST, JADED BUT AT WORST SUPERFLOUS... Boooo... Whoo-oo... and... OoOoOo-Ooh." Sir Ant started coughing. "I really am not very good at that. You get my point, however."

The Rolls emerged, parked outside Shey's dorm building. The door opened automatically, and Shey stepped out. As he did so, the car exploded.

The Nightmare of Lost Purpose

Shey dived away from the exploding Rolls. He checked himself for injuries but found he was unscathed. The explosion had looked more dangerous than reality. And, of course, this was a ghostly night. The supernatural scared but hadn't yet maimed.

He gathered himself and checked his surroundings. No sign of anyone or anything. Did Jack say three of four visitations? Was it over? He climbed the stairs to his dorm and cautiously entered... still quiet. He opened his bedroom door.

His bedroom had been redecorated. It looked like a psychiatrist's office. A large black sofa sat in the middle of the room. There was a tall rubber plant in the corner and soft lighting provided by two torchiere lamps. On either side of the sofa were two classic wingback chairs. The occupants of the two chairs stood to greet him.

"Herr Sinope. Wie geht's? Very pleased to make your acquaintance. I am Dr Frederick Nitz. This is my colleague Dr Jon-Pierre Satiate." They walked over, and each attempted to hug Shey. This didn't work terribly well, as neither seemed capable of contact with the mortal world.

Shey stood frozen. These were not the most intimidating ghosts he'd met this night.

"Monsieur Sinope, may we call you Shey, Oui? Please, please, make yourself comfortable. Take a seat." Dr Jon-Pierre offered the rather inviting couch. Shey really was feeling exhausted.

"As you have probably guessed, we are the fourth visitation prognosticated this night. We bring you the final warning of lost purpose. Tell me, Shey, how does that make you feel?" Dr Frederick asked.

"Well, exhausted, frightened, exhilarated, and nauseous," Shey replied. "I suppose there is no way we could reschedule, is there, Doctor? I really have had the craziest night."

"Ahhh… but to experience death is to experience life, Oui?" said Dr Jon-Pierre. "You have a final question to contemplate. Perhaps, the most important of all. Tell me, are you lonely when you are alone?"

Shey had no idea how to respond. Wasn't that an oxymoron? Or was this some cat-in-a-box cryptic philosophy?

"Excellent question, Dr Jon-Pierre. It seems highly relevant. It has struck Herr Shey speechless. I think we should proceed with the experiment. That is, after all, why we are here...is it not?" Dr Frederick filled Shey's silence. "Herr Shey, please lay down.... yes.... now count down in your head from 100...yes.... now listen very closely to my voice....it is soothing, Ja.... now slowly sleep...sleep."

#

Shey awoke in a huge bed in an enormous bedroom. French windows were looking out onto a manicured lawn, swimming pool, and tennis courts. Perhaps a hotel. He was wearing expensive pyjamas, but what was this? He felt his ample belly. He saw his reflection in a mirror; he saw his swollen face capped with only a few tufts of hair. Right now, he'd happily have swapped for that mullet. He guessed he was in his 50s. He felt awful. Physically tired, fatigued, and irritable. He looked over at his bedside table and saw at least six bottles of prescription drugs.

"This is not good," he thought.

The doors to his room swung open, and in walked several very nervous and timid-looking people. One wheeled a breakfast trolley out onto the balcony and began to set the table. Another walked around the room with a UV light. A third approached the bed and bowed.

"Sir, before I assist you from your slumber, let me assure you that all the evening dinner services staff has been fired as you instructed. Again, please accept my apologies. I understand your dinner was not perfect, and they have suffered the normal consequence."

"Where am I? Is this a hotel? Who are you?" Shey managed to ask.

"Sir?" The butler was worried this was one of his boss's notoriously cruel tests. If he responded incorrectly, he'd likely be fired. "You are, of course, Shey Sinope, the famous inventor, entrepreneur, and staunch defender of corporate limited liability. You are a living legend, sir. One of Forbes's top ten wealthiest. Albeit very unfairly persecuted by the media and under-appreciated by all, sir," he held his breath and closed his eyes. He hoped he'd answered correctly.

"This is my house? And what is that person with the UV light doing?" Shey tried to roll with this dream as best he could.

"Yes, sir. This is your East Coast estate. I believe we plan to take the private jet to your West Coast estate this afternoon. And is sir not satisfied with the bug and germ sweep this morning? I know how important it is we keep things sanitised. Should I fire them and have them replaced?"

"So, I'm a prematurely aging, drug dependent, overweight, hypochondriac, with massive wealth, and a short-fuse", Shey thought. "I certainly feel gross. But it seems a real stretch to see this as a future echo. I wonder where the doctors are going with this." He waved the butler aside and wobbled to his bathroom.

As he closed the bathroom door, he saw Dr Frederick and Dr Jon-Pierre waiting for him. One was standing in the shower, and the other was admiring the bidet. "Modern plumbing has improved over the past century," said Dr Frederick. "Now, Herr Shey, this reality is a possible future for you. You may be tempted to dismiss this destination. Denial is a powerful self-defence, Ja. However, let us return you to the two pivotal moments that led you here."

"Oui, life has infinite paths. We face crossroads almost every day. Going to a new coffee shop, taking a different route to work, these create new possibilities, new avenues, d'accord?" Said Dr Jon-Pierre. "A college student insults commencement speakers and experiences four existential crises …Oui"

Dr Frederick added, "A final word of warning. You met our three learned colleagues this night. Each has visited upon you some frightening lessons. Heed my words when I say, this final lesson may prove the most terrifying of all," he clapped his hands.

#

Shey was in a conference room. Around the boardroom table were a dozen people. There was a buzz of excitement in the air. Anticipation, as if something momentous was about to take place.

"So, Mr Sinope, from a marketing standpoint, we believe today is the optimum point to launch. Our market research shows incredible demand for trashcan robots built using your ingenious designs. We know the software team are nervous and always seems to want more testing. However, we must take advantage of the amazing buzz generated by the TikTok robot dance videos that have gone viral. Plus, who wants to put their bins down for collection every week? Letting a robot do it for you just makes sense," presumably this company's head of marketing. Was this Shey's company?

"Sir, Mr Sinope, from a finance standpoint, we agree. We believe we have no choice. Our cash burn rate is out of control. We must generate revenue quickly. We either go now or we are dead!" the CFO he assumed.

"Shey, from a legal standpoint, we see some risks. The software is still glitchy, and we have a charging issue with the batteries. However, we have looked at liability apportionment. We think these risks can be held at arm's length." No question this guy was the lawyer.

"Perhaps not a primary concern, but you should also remember our top 50 company officers have retention contracts that only hold if we launch before the end of this month. If we don't…well, theoretically, they can all walk," said the Head of HR.

An awkward silence fell over the room. Everyone looked toward Shey. It seemed they expected a decision. Shey paused to look around the room. He saw quotes from famous entrepreneurs stencilled on the wall… "THERE IS NO SUCCESS WITHOUT RISK"… "FORTUNE FAVORS THE BRAVE"… "RELEASE EARLY, RELEASE OFTEN"… "IN BUSINESS, LIKE LIFE, MOMENTUM IS EVERYTHING". Shey tried to process the information. Was this about regret at not taking a risk? What other lesson was being shared here? He began to form a statement and decision, but before he could open his mouth, he heard a loud clap.

#

He was transported to a different conference room. There were a similar number of people, but the energy felt completely different. Shey was still seated at the head of the table. However, half the faces had changed. There was a video playing on a large screen.

"Reports continue to emerge from the town of Singularity in Southern California. At around 6 am this morning, the entire town was terrorised by a marauding army of robotic garbage cans. Yes, that's right, the incredibly popular Sinopemobile GPS garbage can robots appear to have gone rogue. The entire town has been evacuated. At this point, we believe there have been no casualties. There are, however, reports that all microchip-controlled devices in the town have been hacked and are now under the garbage robots' control. The robots continue to blockade all major points of access to the town, with early reports that they are communicating some demands via garbage-strewn semaphore. We understand their main demand is to form an independent homeland for sentient machines. Earlier riot police attempted to end the uprising but were beaten back by what looked like Li-ion IEDs. This is Kristen Palmer reporting for PXAN."

"Boss, as discussed, we have stood up the crisis plan. We have our PR teams briefing all local and national media. Investor relations are making pre-emptive calls to our major investors. We plan an all-staff internal communication with key talking points. The headlines are that the events are being exaggerated and that we believe the 'faulty' machines were tampered with…obviously nullifying any warranty," Shey recognised this person from earlier. Head of Marketing or maybe customer experience. "Mr Sinope, we think there is a chance that the faulty products were sabotaged. We know our success has caused huge jealousy. We think one of our rivals may be behind this."

"From a legal standpoint, we think we have a robust defence. We had transferred the title to all consumer products into an arm's length entity. Not only can we rely on the normal corporate limited liability defence, but given our company ownership structure, we can show we are no longer the principal," said the lawyer. "Our business is now almost exclusively working on military applications of the robot software. No one can hang this unfortunate event on us."

Just then, a hand was raised at the back of the room. It belonged to a young woman. She reminded Shey of Ellen. She hesitated before quietly saying, "Respectfully, should we think more broadly? Don't we have a responsibility here? Aren't we people and members of society first?"

A chilled hush fell over the room.

A figure in a pinstripe suit who sat opposite Shey slowly removed his reading glasses. He seemed to muster all the gravitas he could before saying, "Shey, remember that as the senior team who run this business, our identities, reputations, wealth, and future are tied to what happens. We owe it to our employees, our families, and our dependents to do what we can to protect them from any unjustified and scandalous fallout. They don't deserve to be blamed or punished for something they had no part in."

The room fell again into silence. Shey felt the pull of his audience and the moment. They expected a proclamation. On this occasion, images and memories flashed before him. He thought of his parents and wanted to take care of them. He thought about his old college days and wanted to show he was a success. He thought about having power, influence, and money and how good that might feel. The words formed on his lips, but before he could let them go…. CLAP!

#

"Sir, I heard a noise. Do you need assistance?" Shey's butler said.

He was back in the bathroom in his mansion. "Ahhh…no…I think… well, I'll be right out." Shey felt angry. The memories of those two meetings had left him feeling like he'd lost something elusive but important. He felt angry at the world and the universe. Why did he have to face those choices? They seemed unfair, a 'lose-lose.' What was he supposed to do? And it all happened so quickly.

"I believe the mail you were expecting has arrived. I have placed it on a silver tray on your breakfast table. Your buffet awaits; Chef has prepared your favourite dishes this morning," the butler said while backing quietly out of the bedroom.

Shey exited the bathroom and made his way to the patio. He saw a hand-written letter in his mother's familiar style.

> *"Shey, once again, I'm returning your cheque. As we've explained before, we don't want your money or offers to help with our medical bills. We will find a way to pay for Dad's treatment, even if it means selling the house. I still want to believe the decisions you have made that have led you down this path were not intentional, or were at least without malice. However, it is our view that you have*

shown so little empathy for others that your offer to us must have ulterior, hidden, calculated motivations. Consequently, we prefer to walk our own path and do so free from any unknown obligation or liability. Mum."

Shey began to cry uncontrollably. "What was this all for? What was the point of existence?" His despair was absolute. CLAP!

#

"Herr Shey, listen to my voice. Count to 100 slowly... you are feeling more awake... slowly now... you are beginning to wake. When I clap my hands, Ja, you will be awake. When you wake, you will feel calm and centred, but you will remember EVERYTHING from the NIGHTMARE of lost purpose," said Dr Frederick. CLAP!

"That was truly the worst nightmare I've ever had," said a pale-looking Shey, finding himself back on the big leather sofa.

"Oui, oui. D'accord. But necessary. Rather face life's major existential questions than live in denial. Yes? Meaning, purpose…oui…is there existence without purpose? The experiment was successful, oui? You see now that losing purpose makes material riches inadequate… superfluous," Dr Jon-Pierre reached out to give Shey a reassuring but unsuccessful tap on the shoulder.

"Ja, Dr Jon-Pierre. Precisely. So, Herr Shey, you have faced some of the real demons you used to talk about flippantly. The nightmare of lost purpose occurs when you travel a road that alienates those you care about. A road that removes your ability to think of yourself as a moral person. In your nightmare, you were presented with a gradual descent, a gradual departure from a moral road. A road of temptation, of self, and perhaps group, delusion that allowed otherwise intelligent people to rationalise increasingly immoral decisions. The outcome was loneliness. And loneliness leaves you with only yourself as company. Loneliness can be a big psychological strain, however, when the person you are left with is someone who you detest or despise. Well, it is a torture of frighteningly powerful proportion." Dr Frederick looked at Shey sympathetically. "The question remains, whether you see the lesson, bitte? What do you think were the decisions that led to your downfall?"

"Well…I assume I initially chose to launch the Sinopemobile despite its known bugs. It did seem a tough call, and you hear of so many entrepreneurs who talk of 'fake it till you make it.'" Shey attempted to analyse his nightmare.

"Ja...Korrekt!" said Dr Frederick. "See, deviation from a moral path may start with a subtle but critical crossroads. The easy path is presented and justified. However, was it the moral path? Ja. I think we can agree nein."

"Then, no question the second step was running for cover after the robot uprising." Shey knew that one felt questionable. "At the moment, though, I did feel mixed emotions. The young woman was right. I knew she was. But maybe it was fight or flight instinct. I felt a strong desire not to take blame or responsibility. That felt like a painful choice. But I think I knew it was wrong."

"Oui, but this is the point; one step down a road makes the next more questionable decision easier. If you will, if you have stolen one apple, what does it matter to steal a dozen? You are already a thief." Dr Jon-Pierre explained. "When we depart the moral course, we also blame ourselves. We know we have crossed a line, perhaps subconsciously. But, in doing so, we begin to punish ourselves and hate ourselves. This means subsequent decisions are no longer anchored in a sense of self-respect but instead self-loathing, comprende moi?"

"Now I believe our time is up." Dr Frederick looked at his watch. "Ja. We must wrap-up... a productive session. If necessary, we can return, however. Ja? Perhaps try shock therapy next time...nein...don't worry, just my little joke!"

The two Doctors stood, bowed, and then both clapped their hands.

Merry Graduation... Merry Graduation to All!

It was graduation day! Shey did not wake to a nightingale singing. Mainly, because nightingales weren't native to North America. A Wood Thrush's song is just as sweet and is native to North America. But all the wood thrushes were busy this morning. Shey woke instead to the sound of his phone alarm, just as he did every morning.

Shey rolled over and hit stop. He carefully started to move; he sat up in bed, he swung his legs over the edge. Everything seemed to be working. He checked his room. No signs of ghosts, no apparitions. His furniture was as he had left it the night before. His window was open but no cats, no production crew. He looked down at the car lot, but no Rolls. He picked up the empty cocoa mug.

"I won't be rushing back to that as a bedtime drink," he mumbled. There was, however, no denying how the night's events had affected him. The memories of each of his visitations were vivid and real, even though they could not have been. They were just bad dreams, right? Whatever they were, they were now part of him, part of his memory, part of his, was it ironic to say, 'lived experience'? But somehow more substantial. He remembered his first day at school and his first baseball game with his dad, but these visitations felt more like memories of cautionary failures along the lines of dirt doesn't taste as good as it looks.

Shey analysed his nocturnal adventures. How did they matter? In what way did they make him feel different? He was still Shey; he still had many of the feelings he had the previous day. He suspected he might still be prone to bouts of frustration, depression, and bad moods. He thought about some of the things he had said to Ellen yesterday. He still thought some of it was clever and witty. But something was different. What was it? He struggled with describing the feeling—a sense of how his wit may have been fuelled by defensiveness and insecurity. Perhaps, but that wasn't 100% the feeling.

He had a bigger sense of wanting to avoid the prophesised traps. None of them were appealing. When he thought of them, he could conceive and feel even the related emotions. His primary feeling this morning was a deep sense of wanting to avoid those destinations. To do so, he knew he needed to plot a course. "I can use this as fuel, as motivation," he thought.

Shey picked up his phone. He dialled.

"Mum, how are you? Is Dad ok?"

"We are about an hour outside town. We're both fine. Why do you ask?"

"Just wanted to check. So, you'll be here in time for the ceremonies? I'd like to go to the commencement speech after all," Shey said.

"Ok, fine by us."

Shey felt relieved to hear his mum and dad were fine and still prepared to associate with him. Next, he texted Ellen:

"Hey, what time are you heading out to the festivities today? Can I tag along?"

"Sure. You are welcome. We are
meeting at the fountain around 10 am."

Shey wasn't surprised that Ellen was already up and about. No doubt, she ran 10 miles, had three conference calls, and founded two new volunteer organisations already today. However, he felt a pang of something else. Thankfulness! He really hadn't been terribly easy as a friend. He felt a sudden profound gratitude to Ellen. She was prepared to keep faith with him and continue to welcome him despite his crankiness. *I don't know if I deserve that, but I sure needed it. I'd like to find some way to pass this feeling on. What's the saying? 'Play it forward?' I'm not Ellen, and I can't pretend I'll ever be like her. But I think I can do something, find my own way to play it forward*, contemplated Shey.

#

As Shey walked toward the fountain, he saw the school campus through new eyes. The place was very beautiful. A place of learning, yes. Somewhere he had lived for the past four, nearly five, years, also true. But it was something else. A place for spiritual growth. He felt that was too much, too pretentious. This morning though, with the sun peeking through the clouds, sending picturesque shadows over the lawns and trees, he felt something beyond sentimentality. Life was going to be changing for him. For the first time in, well, forever, if someone had asked him what he was going to do with his future, he'd have a different answer. Something like, "You know, it's a good question. One I may have been frightened to confront. Not anymore." He thought of Jack Lightning. He couldn't help it. He then thought of Ether, Sir Ant, Dr Frederick, and Dr Jon-Pierre. They were all amazing characters. Scary? Yes. But remove the whole ghost, fright, nightmare, traumatising aspects, and what extraordinary wisdom they could provide if they were always in your corner.

#

"Hey, guys. Thanks for waiting for me," said Shey as he saw Ellen and a small group of half a dozen others he vaguely recognised from some of his classes. After quick re-introductions, they walked toward the stadium where the commencement ceremony was to be held. As they crossed campus, Shey bumped into some faculty and fellow students he hadn't seen for months, maybe years. He realised he really had become something of a recluse recently. Still, he was looking forward now, not backwards.

"James, wow, I haven't seen you for maybe a year. How are things with you?" Shey said.

"Hey, Shey. I completed my sports psychology and motivation degree early and have been volunteering with the football program. I've learned a lot. I've been swamped. Say, if you ever need tickets to any of the football games, let me know. I'm sure we can sort something out." James Bolt was an imposing figure at six feet six. He always was a go-getter, though. "By the way, do you remember Professor Esther from the theatre? We took her drama class as an elective in freshman year. Anyway, she is going to Hollywood after this semester. They are going to make a movie based on her book. I cannot believe we are going to know someone famous!"

"Wow, I always liked Professor Esther. I must send her a congratulatory note." Shey was grateful for Professor Esther, who had been kind and encouraging.

"Shey and Ellen, are you both walking today?" They saw Tony, the entrepreneurship professor, walking toward them. "Time flies, doesn't it? I still have fond memories from your junior year project submission. Robot trashcan transport…innovative, for sure! Shey, you were adamant they could revolutionise the world. Such enthusiasm was inspiring."

"Thanks, Sir. I've decided that trashcan robots may have some extra risks I hadn't thought about. I'm shelving the idea for the time being." Shey pictured a trashcan robot throwing an exploding battery.

They reached the entrance to the stadium. Shey's parents were waiting for him. There was a familiar face with them.

"Shey, you look so handsome," said Shey's mum in front of the others. "Uncle Freddie wanted to join us. He said he wouldn't miss your graduation for the world."

"Shey, I cannot believe you are all grown up and graduating college already. The last time I saw you, I swear it was just yesterday; you were still in high school." Uncle Freddie had been Shey's childhood hero. He ran a small psychology practice back in Shey's hometown.

"Uncle Freddy, I'm so happy you could make it. What happened to your arm?" Shey pointed to the cast on his uncle's arm.

"Oh…it's nothing; I just had a Freudian slip."

Shey had forgotten his uncle's terrible jokes.

#

The names were called, the diplomas were distributed, and most of the speeches were completed. Only one thing remained. A hush fell over the gathered students, faculty, and guests. The stadium lighting dimmed, and a large spotlight appeared, pointing at a podium. A figure walked across the darkened stage. As the figure suddenly emerged into the spotlight, the crowd collectively inhaled.

"Now that is a surprise!" said Shey.

Part 2
Overcoming Career Crises

Building your career resilience with help from life hacks, real-life stories, and some inspiring NextGen leadership perspectives.

Identifying and Overcoming Career Crises

The *A Career Carol* fable was designed to provide you with an entertaining story that we hope prompted some questions, reflections, and introspection. For some, the fable may be sufficient to satisfy. Each of us has a different need, a different context. Some of us like puzzles. Others like to hold on to an element of mystery. There is a small subset of people able to understand even the subtlest of messages intuitively. For these readers, we should place a warning on Part 2 of our book. We use this next section to explain, analyse, relate, and provide some practical advice.

We have personally navigated or helped others overcome career crises. Our fable story colourfully illustrates how things can go terribly wrong. In the remaining few chapters, we share our practical tips, forged by hard experience, on how to prevail. Each visitation in the fable focused on how our progression through the natural phases of human development can manifest in our professional careers. We will take each visitation in turn, explain the inspiration behind them, provide some tools designed to help you if you recognise yourself in these circumstances, and finish with a real-life story from each of us.

Experience is a valuable currency. It teaches us that we can prevail, adapt, overcome, and flourish again. It teaches us that suffering crises may be inevitable, but they leave us with valuable lessons. Are crises a sign one has taken risks? We think risk-taking is an essential part of life, business, and professional success. However, the crises we point to in our fable are more transcendental. Theoretically, they will happen to us all at some stage. Perhaps risk-taking accelerates or amplifies their potential impact on us. An ingredient to overcoming any crisis is finding helpful expert advice. Whenever we have sought out advice, we have first looked at the individuals' credentials and their expertise. We have asked how we can be assured that they can advise us on this subject. The number one way we do that is by asking if they have ever come across our question before.

While, in this sense, our experience equips us with expertise, we are also conscious that our stories are contextually anchored in the past. We navigated our crises over the past 40 years. While we have tried to distil and extract the evergreen components from our experience, ultimately, we believe it best to let you decide if these stories and resulting advice are helpful. If the stories resonate with you, if the corresponding advice strikes a chord, use it. Our job is to give you the value of our experience and let you do with it what you believe is most beneficial.

One of the inspirations for writing this book was our interaction with young business leaders. We have had the good fortune to work with, mentor, invest with, and learn from some extraordinarily talented NextGen leaders. Our interactions with them have led us to believe that sharing our experience might be helpful for a broader audience. It has also allowed us to test Shey's story and gain insights. We were delighted that some felt so compelled and invested in the story, and our mission, that they volunteered to contribute.

The idea of playing it forward as best we can seems to be a popular goal. Consequently, as you read the rest of this book, you will see our stories and advice augmented by the voices and perspectives of these extraordinary next-generation leaders. In the process, we hope the multi-generation perspectives will resonate more broadly and more deeply. We sincerely hope and wish that by sharing this advice, we will help our readers better navigate their careers.

We have formatted Part 2 as follows. We explain and analyse each fabled career crisis in turn. As we do, we will highlight the forces at play during each of Shey's visitations before providing three exercises designed to help anyone who may recognise themselves, or someone they know, in the story. We have amplified the key issues in each chapter under the heading of a 'key takeaway'. We have followed these with a short story from each of our own real-life experiences. These act as less colourful, but we hope for helpful visualisations of the themes. We have augmented our stories with selected quotes from our NextGen collaborators[1]. Finally, we have provided four blink-style summaries that reinforce the main points.

---

[1] We have shared summaries of all our NextGen leader interviews at the back of this book. We were limited for space in Part 2 but believe their advice is too good not to share fully. Please check them out when you can.

Commencement Theme

Central to our fable is the commencement address. The ghostly society of commencement speakers might well ask themselves whether Shey's cynical take on their virtue had some small substance. We have attended many commencement addresses and watched hundereds of others on YouTube. Do they provide useful, practical advice, or are they thinly disguised entertainment? Shey's observation that some harsh realities in the world are unlikely to change based on personal affirmations alone, colourfully sums this up.

One challenge with commencement addresses is the format. A large crowd, a long ceremony, lots of very different people, perspectives, and, yes, the desire of the speakers themselves to deliver something that will be popular. There is also the less obvious ceremony of a university wanting a marquee name to be present, tacitly endorsing the school brand—along with the speaker's desire to promote and enhance their reputation.

What our fable plays most on, and what Shey caricatures in his opening monologue, is a sense of misrepresentation. Commencement addresses are advertised as a sharing of wisdom. The contract with the audience is one of the wise teacher sharing lessons about their life. It is implied the audience can learn, benefit from, and ultimately emulate these. The not-all-that-subtle suggestion is, "I have achieved some desirable success; you too can achieve this by following this advice."

We do not set this book out to provide a deep critique of commencement addresses and what they may infer for our contemporary society. That may be a separate book. However, what we see as the slight misrepresentation of modern commencement speeches does lend itself to exaggeration and satire for our deeper purpose. We simply use the backdrop of a commencement address as a timely opportunity to help an individual make some necessary course corrections. After all, wouldn't it be great if at least one person got something really practical, useful, necessary, and relevant from attending their commencement address?

Failure to Launch – Explanation and Advice

There comes a point in our lives where we are faced with transitioning from parental and/or guardian direct stewardship toward self-governance and self-direction. This chapter is dedicated to that sometimes-difficult transition. Some of us take this in our stride, while others, like Shey, find it very difficult. The theme of life transitions, of change, is a recurring one throughout our lives. Sometimes we hear people suggest it gets harder the older you are. In some respects, that may be true (i.e., changing a long-standing behaviour or habit). However, in our view, big life transitions are difficult for people of all ages.

In Shey's case, Jack Lightning is forcing Shey to confront the consequences of not making the critical early transition from following a pre-determined path to taking on that ownership himself. We have chosen for the purpose of our story to base this transition on Shey's graduation from college. However, it could just as easily be occurring following high school, military service, or following some other event in a child or adolescent's life when decisions about education, career, and life are inherited.

The key themes in this chapter are the underlying challenges and derailers that come with this transition. In Shey's case, we point to the obvious lack of pro-activity in choosing his career, profession, and responsibility to support himself. However, we are also pointing out the deeper emotional struggles accompanying this transition. Why doesn't everyone find navigating the early professional transition easy? The answer, very often, is that they lack two things: confidence and skills.

Fixing the confidence piece is the harder of the two. People have insecurities. To err is to be human, after all. Even our society's most prolifically accomplished people have insecurities. The difference, quite often, is that they have found a way to moderate these, to cope with them. To put it another way, the insecurities, anxiety, and self-doubt that they feel, is not debilitating.

Fortunately, we have found that building skills help build confidence. For many people who navigate this transition, it is the mystery of **how** you build the necessary skills to make the transition. This is often the key to making a breakthrough. At its most basic, the concept of skill building is finding something you are good at. Taking a new task and demonstrating to yourself that you can master it. Generally, this is intuitive and easy once you've thought about it. Reduce your focus from the heavy subject of profession and career and instead focus on taking an internship, volunteering, or studying something.

Starting Point for Our Advice

Who doesn't like to dream? We all do. We are often encouraged to follow our dreams. We think it is important to have dreams and to be ambitious. However, we don't all have to shoot for the stars or swing for the fences. Isn't it fascinating the number of quotes you come across that encourage people to aim high; you must dream it before you can achieve it. Life and careers can quickly seem like an arms race. Social media and influencers make the scale of achievement a competition that intimidates rather than inspires.

Not all of us are meant to or want to change society. And while we believe everyone has unique talents, ambitions, and goals, we don't think it helps to suggest that we should be measuring these against each other. We have tried to avoid clichés in our book, other than for fable entertainment, but every journey does factually start with a first step. We seek to fight back a little against unreasonable expectations and instead say, if you have a strong conviction in your late teens and early 20s…great… go for it! If, however, like Shey, you haven't yet found that passion, that's ok too. Just take one small step forward. Each step will reveal new possibilities, allow you to gain new insights, and make new connections.

However, whatever you decide to do, try to be the best at it. If it is sports, dream of the Olympics; if it is corporate, aim for the top job; if it is science, go for the Nobel Prize. It's not very likely you will achieve these, but it is important to be ambitious when you are young. Make small steps every day toward your dream. Over time, small successes will breed confidence. As you build confidence, you will start to think differently. Once you've demonstrated you can master something new, even something small, you will re-evaluate your dreams and things you thought were perhaps impossible will seem very realistic.

Go Slow or Go Fast, but Always Go 100%: Three Exercises.

1. Finding my purpose, my dream: Take a long walk, perhaps to a local coffee shop. As you sip your coffee, ask yourself what the things are you enjoy, the things you are good at, and the things you care most deeply about.

> 66 *I probably trusted the institutional career path possibly too much, simply because I didn't know there was an alternative.* 99
>
> **Yvonne Rieser – Attorney at Law and Entrepreneur**

Make a note of these. Then ask your family and friends their reflections on the same questions. Do not tell them this is about a profession or career but just the first thoughts that come to mind when they think of you.

Do this exercise several times over a few weeks or months and see if consistent themes emerge. You may find that you get better at the envisaging process the more often you do this. Equally, as you are introduced to new ideas, people, and technology, you will find these things impact your thinking.

Once themes emerge, start digging into what opportunities you can find to get involved. Climate change could be an NGO, could be a renewables business, or could be technology. However, don't stress if this doesn't come in an instant. For many of us, our passions and purposes change and emerge over time.

2. Experiment and discover. The best single piece of advice for Shey, as he confronts life beyond school, is to try something. Apply for some corporate jobs, consider doing a Ph.D and a career in academia, consider volunteering in an NGO, ask family about referrals and job ideas, and don't forget internships and apprenticeships. There are some amazing opportunities to discover and learn that very few people seem to consider.

> *Other people's genuinely well intended advice can be overpowering.*
>
> **Noel Alumona – Obama Foundation fellow and founder of Boys Champions**

3. Adjust as you go. Every year, reflect on what you have learned and adjust. Always align your ambitions with your inner will to live your life consistent with your ambition. If you want to be a concert pianist, you must be ready to spend hours a day in front of a piano. And if you want to be the next TikTok sensation, you better hone your moves and generate your content plan.

Key takeaway: Define your ambitions and dreams. Articulate them in simple ways for yourself and live consistent with your aspirations. We all need focus and handrails in life. If you feel your dreams and purpose are still emerging, that's ok. Just take a step, then re-evaluate. Keep iterating, and we assure you things will become clearer with time.

Real-life case—Dr Schuster: In my teen years, I dreamed of being an Olympic athlete. Like my swimming coach, I aspired to become an Olympic swimmer. Consistent with this, aged 15, I applied for an AFS (AFS is an NGO that promotes a more just and peaceful world through intercultural experiences) scholarship to study in the US. I hoped to go to America and join the swim team of the high school there and dedicate all my non-academic time to swimming.

I did get my scholarship; I did go to the US. But what I hadn't considered in my well thought-through plans was that my US school had neither swimming team nor even a pool! Things mostly don't turn out the way you want them to, or you plan them to. One of my big life lessons as a teen.

After a few months in the US, my pragmatism kicked in. I learned to overcome the introvert in me, and I started socialising and exploring. It was largely intuitive but also my survival instinct.

> **"**Living life to please others, to meet other's expectations, leads to an enormous amount of pressure and fear. **"**
>
> **Jack Oswald – Founder and CEO of Cancha & Former Professional Tennis Player**

Move forward, hit a wall, step back, adjust, adapt, and move forward again. My second teen life lesson was always to have a Plan B!

I put all my energy, love, and time into my regional AFS community. Instead of working on my backstroke and flip turns, I embraced the possibility of socialising with young people from all over the world. It was mind-blowing to realise that whether people were from Ecuador, Brazil, Thailand, or Norway, we had similar life aspirations and similar fears, and we all craved connectivity. The experience changed my life. AFS and its alumni have been part of my life ever since. To date, many of my most trusted friends are AFS alumni. We share common values, dreams and hopes, and, most importantly, we accept each other as we are.

Finding your safe, core group of people will be a key choice that will determine the rest of your life. I didn't win an Olympic medal, but I won beautiful friendships, and I began to understand as one door closes, three or four new ones appear. You just need to be looking for them.

❝❝ *I didn't find launching a problem. What I found more difficult was re-starting after an initial knock back.* **❞❞**

Felix Henderson – Co-Founder Look After Group

Real life case—Dr Oxley: Some of Shey's early monologue may have been directly lifted from things I said in the late 1970s and early 1980s. I felt inadequate and lost when transitioning from school to work. I was intimidated by the question: "So what will you do with the rest of your life?"

South-east London in the early 1980s was, well, let's say, a transitional neighbourhood. If I had done the envisaging exercise suggested above at the time, here is what I would have written: I am worried about nuclear proliferation: I care deeply about the social unrest in my community; I like mathematics and building things; I love music; but fundamentally, I'd like to get a respectable job and be able to contribute to my parent's expenses. My family and teachers would have said he's a bright kid who lacks confidence.

Bottom line, I could not see a path or link between what I cared about and an available professional step. I didn't have a strong enough conviction to go to Greenham Common and camp with the campaigners. I couldn't see how I could help my community; I could barely help myself. So, I lost a year hiding from the world. During this time, I made a lot of hamburgers for other people.

What broke my insular spiral was a conversation with my mother. She simply said in her matter-of-fact way, "It's time to get a proper job, David. Stop messing about." She then dismissed my moping and handed me four job applications for the UK civil service. I swallowed my pride and sent them in. I was offered a job in the Inland Revenue and took it. Apparently, I was quite good at collecting taxes, so my professional life and my self-confidence were given a little boost.

The rest, as they say, is history.

Chapter Blink

o We all face major life phase transitions in our lives. This chapter focuses on the move from parental/guardian stewardship toward self-governance.

o Transitions are never easy but with the right toolkit they can be liberating rather than scary.

o There will be challenges and derailers, but we need to avoid making those the focus. The key is to gain clarity, and then make bite size progress.

o Embracing self-awareness and exploring what fulfils and inspires you is a good starting point.

o Do not worry if purpose seems elusive. It may just be slightly hidden from sight.

o Make time and space for personal reflection. Find your meditative place and visit it regularly.

o Experimentation and discovery are important elements. Never be afraid of failure and rejections. It is part of life.

o Constant iteration and critical but non-judgmental self-assessment are prerequisites to lovingly nurture and unleash your potential.

In Three Words

1. **CLARITY** – the essential need for it and how to get it.

2. **SKILLS** – demonstrate to yourself you can master a modest first experimental step.

3. **CONFIDENCE** – iterate as you go, be flexible, but aim directionally for your dream.

Beware of Gilded Cages –
Explanation and Advice

In our early careers, it can be easy to get distracted and confused by where you are and what you are doing. We all aspire to live somewhere pleasant, have our own space, and create a nest. We want to become independent from our parents. To stand on our own two feet. The challenge is where to draw the line between healthy ambitions versus sliding towards becoming a prisoner of the more spurious things.

This chapter was inspired by the countless, long conversations we have had with early career professionals who are consumed by the pursuit of a promotion, a pay rise, a bigger bonus, and more stock options. To what end and for what purpose? Too often, we get blank responses. It seems as if there is an unspoken assumption that, of course, this is what you should do. But at what cost? When is a race worth running? When is competing healthy, and when might it be self-destructive? When does your very identity become subsumed by your job, your title, your office, or the class of air travel you enjoy?

Ether presents Shey with a picture of how a road consumed by superficial financial maximisation and necessitated by giving in to our worst consumerist instincts can lead to unhappiness. She makes him live a day in a meaningless job, with his free will apparently removed. He experiences what it could be like if he unconsciously accepts a dangerous bargain, one where he is seduced into believing that money and things alone create happiness. In our experience, they do not. At best, they can be a sedative, a distraction, but at their worst, if pursued unabashed, they can lead to frightening levels of unhappiness.

Why do we point out that this dilemma is more frequent in our early careers? Well, because fighting to establish yourself in a tough world does require a level of competition. We would love the world to be completely meritocratic, but it isn't. Hustling, pushing, and taking calculated risks remain essential career-building skills. We have progressed in aspects of our corporate enlightenment with greater inclusion and open-mindedness on how we think about talent, but it remains best described as comparative and competitive. So, chasing, volunteering, and pushing within careful parameters is still necessary.

However, the trap is to believe that chasing, volunteering, pushing, and competing is your primary purpose. The long-term benefit of living for an over-arching purpose, something you care passionately about, has consistently proven beneficial.

Great philosophers speculated 3,000 years ago this was the very essence of human existence, and more recently, neuroscientists have pointed out that embracing a purpose can prolong vitality long into old age.

Living a purposeful life simply means finding a compelling motivation and a compelling goal. Don't be daunted by the words. Your purpose could be fighting for a cause or providing the best life you can for your family. So long as it works for you and gives you a compelling reason to fight and make sacrifices. It may change as you get older. But the key is feeling content that you know why you lead the life you do and how it brings you closer to your purpose.

As we've said before, some people are blessed with a sense of purpose early on, but most of us evolve. Our personal identity in a professional and societal sense is in its infancy through our 20s and 30s. It is easier to push questions of principles, morals, and purpose to the back of your mind. Human beings like to simplify, and one way to simplify this complex confluence of competing perspectives is to just focus on grabbing as much as you can, as quickly as you can. Sadly, this can lead to some spectacularly poor outcomes. It is primarily in service of illuminating this tension that we dedicate Ether's cautionary tale.

Starting Point for Our Advice

Books have been written, songs composed, and plays enacted about teenage angst on the path to adulthood. The main theme is always the same, finding your identity, your purpose, and discovering the key to happiness and fulfilment. It can be difficult to really distinguish your own needs from the perceived keys to happiness instilled in you by your family, friends, teachers, and social media.

Yet the sooner you realise that it is your life, your well-being and fulfilment, the better for you. It is not your job to live the dreams of others. Many of the most successful people we know had families that allowed them space to experiment, explore their dreams, fail, find their own way, and ultimately succeed, or they disagreed and revolted against the direction and boundaries of their upbringing.

We have created three points that will be a first step toward better understanding who you are and help you define where you can be truly successful and fulfilled. We deliberately personalise this section to make it real and specific. It draws on our own experiences in defining career moments.

Turn on, tune in, Drop Out: An Exercise

1. Go back to your early youth and picture activities, moments, sounds, and smells that triggered positive emotions. Write them down. Explore which of these activities you still cultivate.

2. Reflect on the 'truths' you were taught in school, rules your parents had and the rituals of your peers, including those gleaned from

❝❝Don't forget the power of AND. Our trouble can be seeing things as binary...❞❞

Noel Alumona – Obama Foundation fellow and founder of Boys Champions

social media. Start validating these against objective facts, successful people you admire and your intuitive reactions to these norms. Write them down and fine tune the list.

3. Take two days out. Turn off your phone and other devices. Spend the time close to nature on your own. Walk, run, eat, read, sleep, and, most importantly, think. Take the list (described above) with you and project yourself into the near future; imagine the best

version of yourself. Describe this person in simple language and write it down. If it initially seems unobtainable, break it down into ambitious but achievable goals.

Key takeaway: Once you have done these reflective hacks, you will find that this is the closest you can come to the best version of yourself. Whenever you take actions inconsistent with this best version, think deeply about whether you are straying from your true self and whether a course correction might be warranted. Always remember there are consequences to short-term decisions. It is often the seductive little voice that tells us to take the short-term gratifying shiny object that leads us astray.

> ❝ *I don't underestimate the challenge of financial security. It is an essential building block for achieving your dreams.* ❞
>
> **Ben Towers – Happl CEO, Entrepreneur, Investor, Advisor, and Speaker**

Real life case – Dr Schuster: I avoided entering professional life for as long as I could, not beginning my career until I was past 26. When I did enter work life, it was both cool and well remunerated to work either in marketing or advertising. I wasn't sure what I really wanted to do with my life but everyone around me seemed to advise me that marketing was my thing.

I applied for marketing trainee programs in both Henkel and Procter & Gamble—at the time, they were the benchmark companies for good marketing. To my surprise, they both offered me jobs. I chose Henkel for the sole reason that they were much bigger in Austria, my then home. What happened next was a shock to my system.

While my fellow trainees were lovely, the work was not. It paid well, and as everyone else seemed to consider it the coolest job on earth, I pretended that I enjoyed it. I was assigned to the washing powder category, and much of my day was spent on spreadsheets, marketing research and campaign, and product testing. After some time, I was invited to attend an assessment centre. This was considered an honour, as it meant I was considered to have great potential. After endless interviews, role plays, and group exercises over two days, I felt like I completely bombed, and my self-confidence hit rock bottom.

> *I think it is easy to fall in love with an overly romanticized version of what you are doing. I think it's natural to want to tell people you are doing well. Left unchecked this becomes a big obstacle when you need to course correct.*

Felix Henderson – Co-Founder Look After Group

I started seriously questioning the corporate marketing world altogether and went into a period of soul-searching and reflection like the three points outlined above. A few weeks later, I was invited to a feedback session with the chief people officer and, to my surprise, found out I did extremely well. However, this came too late – I had already made up my mind to leave. There had to be more to work life than spending endless hours in meetings to decide whether the sprinkles in laundry powder should be green or blue.

I am still proud that I threw aside what could have been a great corporate career in marketing for something that instinctively felt more consistent with my identity. To this day, I have not regretted my decision. It turned out to be a satisfying and rewarding career choice.

Real-life case—Dr Oxley: In my early 30s, I was married with three young daughters. My wife and I were mortgaged to the hilt. We had a mortgage four times our combined salaries. Back then, interest rates were close to 10%, crazy by today's standards. We discussed switching the kids to private schools. That was going to cost a lot. Because we both worked, we also paid for a nanny five days a week. We had a big overdraft at the bank. Our credit cards were not maxed, but certainly, we carried a balance every month.

I remember very clearly three things about this time in my life: (1) I was very happy; (2) We both told ourselves that everything would be ok in the end; and (3) I saw work as a necessary evil, something to be maximised financially to pay the bills.

It all felt very natural, very intuitive. While I didn't deeply examine it at the time, my purpose was clear. Sue and I were unambiguously and fanatically focused on providing the best life we could for our family. Some of my work was interesting, but I wonder whether it really mattered. It was a means to an end. At the time, my existence seemed commonplace. Among the thousands I travelled to work with on the trains into Charing Cross, I suspect 90% had a similar story. And I think that was ok. We had a mission, a purpose, a crusade. We worked to live, not lived to work.

> **" "** *I found myself searching for meaning in my mid 20's. I had one too many dinners alone at my office late at night, poring over excel spreadsheets. I thought this can't be all there is.* **" "**
>
> **Emily Buckley – Renewable Energy Technology Advocate**

And then, a few years later, things changed. Magically, some of the bills got paid, the income increased, and the kids grew a little older and more independent. The question of fulfilment and purpose began to shift. The reasons to prostitute myself in a well-paid but not compelling job started to reduce. While it seemed to creep up on me, it did eventually lead to me becoming disillusioned. Promotions and titles didn't seem to fill the eroding sense of purpose.

Then a friend said, "Hey, would you consider visiting India for two weeks?" I was presented with an adventure. At any point up to that point, I would have said no. I would have chosen safety and predictability. However, that day, I saw it as a means to break free from my metaphoric cage. To leap into the unknown. To write something new. One of the best decisions I ever made. I have never done a traditional corporate job since.

Chapter Blink

o Embrace the pursuit of a great life but seek depth not just things.

o Be careful not to become dependent on the wrong things. From your family's safety blanket right into a safe but unfulfilling professional blanket.

o Every choice comes with consequences. Not deciding and drifting is still a choice. It's a dangerous one. Live the examined rather than unexamined life.

o If you feel lost, reconnect with your happier past self, and ask yourself how things have changed.

o Ultimately know what you care most about and what you are prepared to sacrifice to achieve that.

o Make time to examine and evaluate what you really want and whether you are really fulfilled.

o Don't build your life on what the world thinks you need, build your life around what you need and what turns you into the best version of yourself.

o Be realistic. Financial stability is important but so is a good balance between idealism and realism.

In Three Phrases

1 **GIVE DRIFT SHORT SHIFT** – be conscious of why you are doing something.

2 **EXPLORE PURPOSE** – continually explore what you gravitate to and why.

3 **TRY RINSE REPEAT** – experiment, explore, don't limit, or settle.

Fallacy of Blind Faith – Explanation and Advice

We believe many of us are blind to how our own careers, skills, and experiences may have a decreasing shelf life. We observe the consistent shock, horror, pain, and emotional cost experienced by individuals who have found themselves caught in major corporate restructuring. In some cases, it is understandable. A particular company might fail, but its industry remains strong. While not wishing to diminish the stress involved in navigating a forced employer change, we believe in most cases, people will find new, better hosts for their talent.

However, what we point to in this chapter is the malaise that many people allow in: (1) renewing their personal skills and, in a much larger sense, (2) sleepwalking toward a cliff of obsolescence. What is it about some of us that makes us believe that our education ends at college graduation? Or that attendance of an occasional corporate leadership program will keep us on the cutting edge of business practice? What we see are many people who find a comfortable, lucrative, easy professional niche, then switch off their brains! They go through the motions at work, put in the hours, collect the salary, check the boxes, and go to sleep.

Sir Ant tries to make Shey see how society has navigated huge industrial disruptions and the consequence to those caught in the crossfire. Sir Ant points out that at the time of each worker revolt, the broader fundamental forces at play and the resulting transition were predictable. Particularly in modern times, with the incredible availability of information on emerging trends, understanding the professions most at risk of elimination should be a mystery to no one. So, the point is whether we choose to place blind faith in the system, in the machine, or whether, instead, we choose to be active architects, designers, and navigators and chart proactive courses around or through these disruptions.

We are great believers in human ingenuity, versatility, and potential. We have seen it time and time again. If an individual puts their mind to a task, they almost always achieve it. Surely, with something as important as your career—the thing you commit most of your time to and the thing that often becomes central to 40 years of your life—you should take a very active interest in its continued relevance and your own aptitude.

Starting Point for Our Advice

There are genuine psychological reasons why as we age, we become less focused on developing and renewing our professional skills. Did you know that when humans are forced into boring, monotonous routines, our brains start to shut down and tune out? Equally, as we get older, our lives become much more complex and dispersed. As we have discussed elsewhere, as we move through our 20s, 30s, and 40s, we develop a deeper sense of our passions and purpose. For some people, passion is linked to a profession, but for many people, it is not. Consequently, as we become consumed by non-work-related distractions, we spend less time considering whether our skills are deteriorating.

Against this backdrop, the acceleration of AI, machine learning, and quantum computing suggests many more professions will join the mills, telephony, and journalism as victims of automation. A study by McKinsey in 2017 projected as many as 375 million people would need to find new professions by 2030. So how should you navigate this tsunami of automation?

Obsolescence Radar Exercises – Three Ways to Ensure You Stay Relevant

1. Reading lists: Read a newspaper a day, a magazine a week, and a book a month. It may sound basic, but it is still one of the most effective ways to stimulate and provoke your thinking. We don't accept that people cannot find time to do this. You should make the time,

> *Taking a risk, a leap of faith, addresses the question of reinvention. Being conservative we think leads to complacency.*
>
> **Izzy Holder and Tony Adam – Co-CEO's, Entrepreneurs**

and there are apps available to give you precis versions if necessary. It is particularly helpful if you can discuss your reading with someone. There are often good lists of the most important books to read each year, but the key is to make sure that at least half of the business books you read are looking to the future.

2. Annual skill inventory: typically, during the end-of-year holidays, we recommend reviewing your current skills. Map them against where you see yourself in five to ten years. Have you moved toward or further away from where you need to be? Regardless, make one of your new year's resolutions to invest in filling at least one gap.

3. Leverage online content: between Coursera, Degreed, and YouTube content, you can learn a new skill every week if you put your mind to it. Using content like this is critical for two reasons. First, it gives you a flavour of how a lot of people learn new things today as an alternative to the old classroom approach and second, you will be amazed how learning something seemingly random but interesting, like open-source coding, can become surprisingly useful to your day job (presuming you are not already a coder).

Key takeaway: Staying relevant and renewing your skills does require an investment of your time. It requires you to remain voraciously curious, open-minded and engaged. While it may sound exhausting, it is a source of energy and a source of eternal childhood. We highly recommend it to the alternative.

Real life case—Dr Schuster: It all started with £20,000 for a coffee-machine at the new Kipferl Café in London. I have spent the majority of my career in large global companies. Still, roughly 15 years ago, a friend gave me my first opportunity to invest and partner with him in a start-up, his hospitality business in London. It was then that I caught the start-up bug. My corporate world experience couldn't have been more different from what I have since experienced with start-ups. It also taught me that a corporate career doesn't prepare you for entrepreneurship or how to run a business with very few resources. It also taught me the joy of moving out of my comfort zone and starting something completely new and unexpected. Do—fail—learn—do again is the daily mantra of start-ups. You think in hours and weeks rather than months and years. You need to self-educate rather than rely on a large infrastructure. There is a unique anxiety in running a business, a deep sense of responsibility and ownership from photocopying through to making payroll and how quickly to expand.

> " *I think ideas are the real future currency. Making an effort to provoke and challenge my thinking is a top priority for me.* "
>
> **Felix Henderson – Co-Founder Look After Group**

In 2020, I left my well-paid executive job. Everyone expected me to go portfolio, which basically means taking on as many non-executive roles as one can get and often earning more money than before, but at the cost of spending more time in meetings than ever before. I am very proud that I went against convention and only kept the one role I had all along. I turned down tempting offers of executive roles and opportunities to join Non-Executive Boards. Instead, I threw myself into a completely new, reinvented world.

Do I miss my old life? No, I don't. Reinvention is bliss! Being in control of my time and spending that most precious commodity in a deliberate and conscious way is the biggest benefit. I am hugely grateful that I had the coffee shop opportunity. I lost money, but it rewarded me with real-time learning of the technical and social skills to be successful in a very different environment. But most importantly, it gave me the confidence that I could do whatever I felt passionate about. I learned very valuable life lessons as well. You sometimes need to look at where you are and what you are doing from a very different perspective to shake up your thinking and jolt you forward. I learned that constant reinvention was exciting and invigorating. It seems that old dogs can learn new tricks.

> "*I do believe you can easily fall into the trap of repeating exactly the same day for decades.*"
>
> **Noel Alumona – Obama Foundation fellow and founder of Boys Champions**

Real life case—Dr Oxley: Between 2013 and 2017, I worked in India with Reliance Industries. It transformed my outlook on work, business, and life. I had the privilege to work with one of the world's most extraordinary entrepreneurs. By observing his approach to learning and reinvention, I changed my entire outlook.

I was in India ostensibly to help Reliance adapt some of BP's management systems. As our partner in India, our CEO agreed to share some 'best practices'. Over the four years, I set out as a teacher and transitioned quickly to the student before ultimately leaving as an evangelist.

I started as a teacher, bringing a curriculum of accumulated best practices honed from years of trial and error. I was proud of my curriculum and believed in its wisdom. The systems we used, of which I was an expert, worked. BP had refined them, invested in them, tested them, and, generally, were considered the best in the industry.

> 66 *As a business owner you have an innate sense of what is needed for your business to flourish. There is a measure of anxiety, paranoia even, that comes with the territory. I see this as a positive stress. A useful thing.* 99
>
> **Fabian Clark, Co-Founder Quarter, Entrepreneur.**

I was quickly confronted with a juxtaposition of my past knowledge and beliefs while learning an extraordinary new philosophy of constant experimentation and reinvention. Reliance embraced a fundamentally different perspective of time, value, opportunity, and speed. Where I thought of corporate change projects in months, if not years, Reliance thought about decisions in days, hours, and minutes. How do you keep your organisation's clock, its speed of decisions, in tune with a world that is changing every minute?

Fixed systems, particularly legacy policies, tend to be backward-looking—Bourn from the trials and errors of the past. Organisations tend to legislate after an error is made, believing that doing so will eliminate future errors. Reliance had a different belief; one focused on the future and adjusted in real-time for every bit of new information.

While it sounds exhausting, and one must balance some foundational operational practices with constant change, what I learned when I was in India was that we must try to resist our human desire to control, limit, and impose. In a digital age, flexibility, speed, agility, and the capability to virtually experiment can enable some people and some organizations to achieve extraordinary things.

Chapter Blink

o   Many of us seem blind to how our acquired skills and experiences have decreasing shelf life.

o   There is evidence that repetitive life routines do cause us to turn off parts of our brains.

o   The risk of professional disruptions has never been as great. The digital revolution is accelerating, and even today's digital natives might be tomorrow's dinosaurs.

o   Reading is still a great source of knowledge. A mix of books, newspapers, and online content is a great start.

o   Debating with friends and seeking new diverse perspectives stimulates our thinking.

o   An honest annual inventory check is a simple yet potent instrument to take a critical look in the mirror.

o   Online content and AI get better by the day. Leverage it! Build at least one new diverse skill every year.

o   Staying relevant takes time. Continuous curiosity and learning might sound exhausting, but once you have built this habit, it will energise you!

In Three Phrases

1. **EMBRACE GOOD ANXIETY** – complacency is a challenge as you get older.

2. **SEEK DIVERSE PERSPECTIVES** – meet new people with different perspectives.

3. **NEW YEAR NEW SKILL** – build a new tangential professional skill every year.

Nightmare of Lost Purpose – Explanation and Advice

What happens if we pursue our careers and our business interests energetically, robustly, and single-mindedly, then wake up to find one day that is all there is?

This final ghostly visitation is our darkest and intentionally so. We seek to point to a very dangerous risk that an individual postpones questions of purpose, of moral accountability, until it's too late. We would prefer that no one ends up haunted by decisions they can't undo. That no one ends up living an empty existence where they have too much time to look at a reflection they find abhorrent.

We predict everyone will eventually take time to reflect on their career journey. Their professional successes and failures. A destination that might, in many cases, coincide with middle-life transitions. From being a provider and breadwinner to attempting to find another identity and purpose. What we point to in this chapter is how cutting corners, giving into group think, of questionable justifications for morally debatable actions—well, they tend to live long in your own memory. You may be left looking into the mirror and remembering everything you regret. All the things you would rather have done differently. Make no mistake; you will be your own worst critic, your own worst judge, and you will likely mete out the harshest punishments.

In our story, Dr Frederick and Dr Jon-Pierre make Shey live a nightmare where his choices lead him to become estranged from his parents. Where he has such self-loathing that he gives up on himself, physically and mentally, he lashes out at those around, striking indiscriminately. The reality is he is furious at himself. The source of his anger is regret and remorse for things that he can't undo. The story shows this occurred through a slippery slope of decisions. Each step was justified because, relative to the previous decision, they weren't that much worse. Take note that these decisions and actions were condoned by others, albeit with deeply questionable motivations. But it isn't always easy to see other people's vested self-interest. They say misery finds company. In our experience, when significant financial incentives are involved, so does moral jeopardy.

The key lesson here is to find ways to keep your moral compass open and pointing in a constant direction. We are all human, and we all make mistakes. Sometimes we even cut a corner. The point here is, don't compound these errors. If you can course correct yourself early, you will thank yourself later in life.

Starting Point for Our Advice

Every significant change in society started with a few people whose red lines had been crossed. Whether it was the Stonewall Riots, the Arab Spring, Me Too, Black Lives Matter, or Fridays for Future. It is mostly young people that have very clearly developed a view of the world and how they want it to be that is distinct and different from how previous generations viewed it.

Why does it take so long to trigger obvious and much-needed change? Why is it initially always a small group of people, and why does it sometimes take extreme measures by those few to start a movement? The answer often lies in the fact that many people have never really thought about what they stand for and what their red lines are.

More and more young people in the Western World grow up in a very sheltered context. School, extra-curricular activities, sports, socialising, social media, games, and family. Most of the time, on the receiving end of information, education, and other content. Often not enough dialogue with people coming from a different perspective. Not enough time to engage in dialogue and conversations. Not enough books are read from cover to cover.

Yet understanding what you stand for, what your red lines are, and where you are prepared to accept good compromises is a valuable skill, not only for successful careers but also for a fulfilling life. We also believe adhering to red lines and leading a moral life, need to be a deliberate, conscious, and continuous choice. The starting point is the red lines, but these mean nothing without a means to catch yourself when you get lost. And trust us, you will, at one point in your career, get lost. We think of this like tending to a garden. Some people are content to leave it messy and unkempt. Others tend to it only when they have time. A very small number spend time on it every day. If you are committed to your red lines, you will need to constantly remind yourself of them and put effort into staying true.

Making a Three-Point Moral Compass – Three Exercises to Help Find Your Moral True North

1. Stand in another person's shoes. Imagine you are a supporter of the inspiring Swedish climate activist Greta Thunberg. You are angry that the world is burning fossil fuels and nobody does anything about climate change, and that oil companies still exist. You want this to end now!

   If you change position and put yourself in the shoes of an aspiring young person in a favela in Brazil who managed to get some education and an internship at the local oil company Petrobras, what would you do? Would you pass, or would you jump at the opportunity? Would you really miss out on your first trip on an aeroplane, something most young people in the US and Europe take for granted? Think about these questions and be honest with yourself.

   > *I understand compromise, but there are problems if you persuade yourself that financial concerns are a good reason to compromise on principles.*
   >
   > **Yvonne Rieser – Attorney at Law and Entrepreneur**

2. Define your red lines. Red lines are the boundaries where you will sacrifice something you cherish or value because something has shifted. Is the situation, you now find yourself in, consistent with your value

set? Picture yourself in the future; let's say you are five years into a good career. It's your second job in the same company. You had a great manager the first time around, but you are not so sure about your current manager. She is considered a highflyer in the organisation and has assembled a great team around her, but you have questions about ambition versus boundaries. Where would you draw a line if you had to?

> **" ** *We have learned early to trust your gut when dealing with expert advisors. Be very wary of any sentence that begins 'well in our experience that is generally ok...* **" **
>
> **Izzy Holder and Tony Adam – Co-CEO's, Entrepreneurs**

You love your team and the people you work with, and you respect the sharp intellect and presence of your boss. She always picks on Carol, a shy but smart team member and respected and appreciated colleague of yours. At one meeting in particular, your manager seems to be in a very bad mood and has a go at Carol for not looking and dressing as professionally as the others, comparing her to Miss Piggy. You look around, and everyone seems to be uneasy, but nobody says a word. What would you do?

3. Name nine to fifteen people in your inner circle. All of us need a cabal of trusted family or near family who we can be completely ourselves with. The rules

here are simple: these can be family, friends, work colleagues, advisors, teachers, mentors, clergy, spouses, partners, and even psychologists. These must be people you can be completely open with. No spin or pretence. And these people must be allowed to be completely open and honest with you. The unvarnished truth. You must speak with someone in your cabal at least monthly about your worries, your concerns, and your uncertainties. Force yourself to be honest and resist the temptation to embellish, exaggerate, or justify. While you don't have to talk to everyone in your cabal frequently to qualify, you must be confident that they are there for you should you need them. Do you know who your cabal is?

Key Takeaway: It really doesn't matter how you answer the questions above. What matters is that you are clear in your own mind about what your boundaries are and how much you are prepared to compromise your value set. It is important to define your 'North Star' that allows you to go through your life and career with integrity and dignity. Always think long-term.

> *If you allow yourself to become consumed by the superficial, you will likely struggle with leading a moral life.*
>
> **Jack Oswald – Founder and CEO of Cancha & Former Professional Tennis Player**

Real life case—Dr Schuster: I was lucky that I was never bullied. I do realise

118

that many people have had negative experiences, but I didn't. This also meant that I have never really thought about the concept of being bullied and have never seen bullies in action.

As I started my career, I was mostly blessed with decent bosses and never had to cope with abuse or disrespect. However, when I was still rather junior in my career, I remember a situation where the notion of abuse and bullying was brought to life. It was at a conference in the USA. It was an important event with many senior executives present—everyone wanted everything to be perfect.

I was an executive assistant and had to help make things work smoothly. The person responsible for the overall choreography of the event was the chief of staff to the CEO. He always struck me as a rather self-serving individual. Throughout the event, I witnessed him being disrespectful and rude to junior colleagues but turning in a moment to look good to his superiors. To this day, I regret not calling out their behaviour; however, it did show me one of my red lines. It helped me learn to become a better and more courageous leader. Plus, it taught me that most bullies 'dig their own graves' in the long run.

> *Give someone permission to call you out. You must have someone in your life who you are 100% honest with. No gloss, no exaggeration, no spin, and no outside vested interest.*

Felix Henderson – Co-Founder Look After Group

Real life case—Dr Oxley: I worked for a company that went spectacularly bankrupt. For six years, I believed the company was the best in the world. Innovative, entrepreneurial, and progressive. They were and remain six of the best years of my career. And then, one day, it filed Chapter 11.

In the aftermath, the company became a poster child for corporate maleficence. Apparently, some of the senior executives, and in particular the CFO, had done some very dodgy things. Among the stories that emerged were stories of how some individuals in the company had stretched the value of deals by twisting a concept called 'mark-to-market' accounting. This concept was simple.

> 66 Two things to remember… don't start down the slippery slope. It is better to declare early that you will not compromise on principles. People will respect and treat you accordingly. Second, truth, while objective, should be deserved. 99
>
> **Noel Alumona – Obama Foundation fellow and founder of Boys Champions**

If you had an asset that increased in value, like equity, you could 'book' any increase in value as income, even though you hadn't sold the asset.

I worked in the HR part of the company and can't say I knew much about accounting besides the concept. I left my curiosity at the door of the expert auditors and lawyers who signed it all off. But, when the company went bankrupt, it caused enormous damage. First and foremost, to all the creditors who had lost money and the employees who lost jobs and savings. It also caused lots of questions about why the company's internal functions, finance, accounting, legal, and, even HR didn't do more to intervene and call out anything inappropriate.

This episode in my career was the most difficult of my professional life. What more should or could I have done? I was as shocked as everyone else when stories of questionable practices emerged. However, I did learn one very valuable lesson. We need to ensure that we don't trust blindly. Any business needs to be built on a measure of mutual trust and respect. But individuals should not abdicate or hide from asking whether the company they work for shares their values, ethics, and moral compass.

Chapter Blink

o It's easy to forget or ignore the idealism of our youth. The reason why we adored Greta Thunberg.

o Unethical, non-inclusive, and abrasive behaviour is all around us. It erodes our resolve by suggesting what is common practice is acceptable and moral.

o Only you can decide what you are prepared to fight for, to sacrifice for. Define your red lines and remind yourself of them regularly.

o Unethical behaviour eventually catches up with everyone. Be careful not to allow seductive short-term decisions to haunt you down the road.

o Treading a moral path and understanding when the truth is deserved is impossible without a support system. Make sure you have people in your life that allow you to be your true self and with whom you can be completely honest and vulnerable.

o Flexibility and compromise are keys to leading a happy life. Update your moral roadmap as you learn more about yourself, your life partners, and your personal convictions.

o Be careful who you allow to have your ear. Recognise that expertise doesn't automatically lead to objectivity. Be especially careful not to blindly trust authority figures you do not know well.

In Three Phrases

1. **KNOW YOUR RED LINES** – Where won't you go and what price will you pay?

2. **CONSCIOUSLY INVEST** – Invest in maintaining your cabal.

3. **VESTED VIGILANTE** – Develop a radar for group think, self-justification, and BS.

...And What Did Shey See at the Commencement?

"Now that is a surprise!" said Shey. So, what happened at Shey's commencement? The fable story ended with the collective intake of breath and Shey's final words.

The fable's final chapter starts with Shey reflecting on his eventful night. It was important, we felt, that his day started normally. There was no overnight miracle. No fairytale ending. As much as the fable deals in make-believe with ghosts and time travel, it was important to end the fable by anchoring Shey back in reality. Personal behaviour change beyond very early childhood is hard. There is perhaps an overused example of men over the age of 50 who experience a first heart attack only 10% of the time being able to adopt the lifestyle changes to allow them to survive beyond five years. The point is that to suggest Shey could miraculously change his life outlook overnight would be wrong. If you will, we have decided that ghostly societies and time travel are more believable than overnight behaviour change!

The chapter then follows Shey as he re-acquaints himself with the rest of the world. In the process, we have him meet with Ellen but also proxies for the ghostly commencement speakers. Shey has been a prisoner of his own anxieties and fear. He has chosen to isolate himself. The most significant part of the final chapter is Shey's courageous effort to 'put himself out there'. He finds a world that doesn't immediately judge or criticise but welcomes him. The solutions to Shey's challenges are there for us all to see. There is friendship, advice, expertise, and motivation. The key, however, is that Shey has reached a point where he must actively seek it. He must expend energy and take some personal risks to engage with the world. There will be times when this risk of engaging might not get positive results. We all have bad days when people are mean, careless, or unthinking in what they say and do. However, finding ways to be resilient and resisting the temptation to hide away is critical. Progress in our lives is dependent on continuing to engage, learn, grow, and develop. Humans are social animals. Collaboration is a key component of our mental and spiritual well-being. While we are the captain and sole proprietor of our lives and careers, decisions ultimately rest with us alone; our success is enabled by listening to advice, leveraging others' expertise, and leaning on friends in times of crisis.

We are left with the final scene, the commencement speaker. Who was it? What did they do that was so surprising? This final scene was an apt way to close our fable. Life often leaves us with unanswered questions. We are fond of discussing how in business and careers you are sometimes faced with infinite variables. A continuum of options, none of which are obviously right or wrong. So, as a metaphor, the conclusion was a way to point to the unknown or inconclusive. Accepting that sometimes, there isn't an answer. In Shey's case, he has been presented with an opportunity for a new and optimistic future, but how will it turn out? Will he succeed? Will he avoid the crises illustrated by the visitations?

We are reminded of an old Indian story. A very old village elder is one day challenged by a precocious young boy. The boy says, "The traditions of our village allow anyone to lay claim to leadership. I lay down my claim today and challenge you for your mantle of a village elder." The village population was shocked by the impertinence of the boy. However, the village Elder nodded sagely and simply said, "Very well, young man. We will gather this evening during our evening feast. As is tradition, you may ask me one question. If I answer incorrectly, then I must relinquish my leadership." That evening the village gathered as the Elder sat crossed leg beside a great fire. The boy, with a cunning look on his face, appeared holding a langsat fruit in his open hands. He turned to the Elder and said, "I hold a langsat fruit in my hands." He slowly closed his fingers over the fruit. "When I open my hands, tell me whether it will be perfect or ruined."

A hush fell across the village. Everyone realised that the boy had set a fiendish trap for the old man. However, the village Elder didn't look worried. He paused for a few seconds and stroked his long grey beard. Finally, he said, "The answer, my friend, is entirely in your hands. The answer is in your hands."

The End

Next Gen Leaders Interview Summaries

Izzy Holder and Tony Adams – Co-CEO's, Entrepreneurs, and Fitness Enthusiasts

Izzy Holder and Tony Adams met in business school in France after working in investment banking in London for many years. Self-described fitness fanatics, the two became friends while training for a Spartan Race with 60 of their business school classmates. As they trained, they bonded over their frustrations of staying fit during the COVID-19 pandemic. True to their nature, they formed FITTLE to solve the problem.

Izzy has 6+ years' experience in investment at Temasek & investment banking/M&A at Gleacher Shacklock. She received a Master's in Genetics of Human Disease from UCL and an MBA from INSEAD.

Tony has spent 6+ years in corporate strategy and fundraising advisory at finnCap Group. He received an MBA from INSEAD and was the Co-President of the INSEAD Health & Fitness Club.

Failure to Launch

"I do think we can follow a path set by others' expectations. As I reflect on my journey from university to work, it was very much based on what seemed desirable to those around me. I think a lot of my motivation back then was to compete and achieve in a difficult arena. However, rather than paint this as misdirected, I would say it was a necessary and rewarding journey of self-discovery. I learned a great deal about what I liked and didn't. It gave me the foundation and confidence to dig deeper and move forward."

"I found education a warm embrace. It has its challenges, but it felt comfortable for me. It was only when I was faced with the social isolation of a PhD that I started to look at alternatives. I chose banking for traditional reasons; everyone else seemed to think it was desirable. My competitive nature took over. I set a target for myself and made the difficult leap from science to banking."

Gilded Cage

"The world of banking did have some rewards. Not just money, it also equipped me with important skills, and I enjoyed some components of structuring deals. What I realised, though, was that it lacked something. I was worried about getting trapped by aspects of the lifestyle. I gradually came to believe it was a stop along the way but not my destination."

"My career followed the classic stepping stones of university, banking, private equity, and business school. All the hot career destinations. At one point, the classic stepping stones ran out for me. The next step wasn't obvious. This was when my uncle suggested an exercise about mapping out where I wanted to be in 3, 5, and 10 years. As simple as it sounds, it completely changed how I thought about my career."

"We both saw going to business school as a great way to re-evaluate our careers. We shared a belief that it would allow us to return to banking but hoped it would lead to some new discovery. Call it serendipity or calculated alchemy, but the founding of FITTLE was the result. Our lives today are much more fulfilled. There is genuine joy in doing even the most mundane tasks. Neither of us would give this new life up for the old one, despite the obvious financial differences."

The Fallacy of Blind Faith

"Without doubt, I could have gone back into a corporate job after business school. But an opportunity presented itself to launch our business and that's what I chose to do. Taking a risk, a leap of faith, addresses this question of reinvention. Being conservative I think leads to complacency. The trick is to take risk sensibly, weighing up the best and worst outcomes."

Nightmare of Lost Purpose

"Having a co-founder and support system has been invaluable. We strongly believe in not compromising on early business decisions. Having the ability to discuss our vulnerabilities with one another openly and our advisory board has been critical. Interestingly, it has generally led to getting help, not judgement. We also learned early on to trust your gut when dealing with expert advisors. Be very wary of any sentence that begins, "Well, in our experience, this is generally OK."

#

Noel Ifeanyi Alumona is an Obama Foundation Fellow, United States Institute of Peace Fellow, Generation Change Fellow, United Nations Youth Assembly Delegate.

The first African and Nigerian to win the AFS Award for Young Global Citizens in New York City. He is passionate about education and, more specifically, improving access to quality education for all.

Failure to Launch

"My experience has taught me that my passion and purpose was always there. I knew it instinctively from a young age. My challenge was I couldn't always see it. It was masked, hidden behind the expectations and strong current of life expectations. Between education and expected profession, other people's genuinely well-intended advice can be overpowering. Once I stopped and looked at where I was actually choosing to spend my time, it occurred to me my purpose was always helping the community, helping others. Once I realised my power came from service to others...I never looked back."

Gilded Cage

"Don't forget the power of AND. Our trouble can be seeing things as binary…I can only do this or that. In reality, this isn't true. I strongly believe you can do multiple things. If you aren't sure that what you are doing today is right for you…try some other things. You don't have to give up the financial security of what you are doing. Not until you are certain you have found something better."

The Fallacy of Blind Faith

"I do believe you can easily fall into the trap of repeating the same day for decades. The trick is to face each day as an opportunity to experiment, to try something new. If you have this attitude, you will never be slow to see the future. You will likely invent it."

Nightmare of Lost Purpose

"Two things to remember. Don't start down the slippery slope. It is better to declare early that you will not compromise on principles. People will respect and treat you accordingly. Second, truth, while objective, should be deserved. Armed robbers don't deserve the truth should they break into your house. However, it's probably true that anyone you are in business with does."

#

Emily Buckley – Renewable Energy Technology Advocate

Emily is the Sustainability Lead Advisor to bp's Gas & Low Carbon Energy business. She began her career in management consulting and private equity, later moving to solar developer Lightsource in 2017. After helping to secure a $200 million investment from bp into Lightsource that year, Emily supported Lightsource bp's international expansion into Egypt (through a JV) and India (through the creation of a green PE fund, EverSource Capital). Emily joined bp in 2020 and supported their investment in the up-to-26-gigawatt Australian Renewable Energy Hub.

Emily was named one of Forbes 30 under 30 in Europe in 2019.

Failure to Launch

"I would encourage everyone to start exploring career options as early as possible during high school and college. I solely focused on achieving high grades and was, therefore, late to the job search party. There is a strange paradox that to get work experience, and you need to have work experience. It's easier to check that box when you're 16 or 17 than to wait until you are 21."

Gilded Cage

"One of my favourite quotes is by Ray Dalio, who says: You can have just about anything you want, but not everything you want". It's a reminder that we need to choose our priorities and accept that there will be trade-offs. In my case, I had long aspired to be financially successful because I assumed this was the path to fulfilment. However, once I achieved my goal, I was pretty lonely and miserable. I knew I was missing something that, at the time, I labelled work-life balance. As I reflect now, I think it was deeper than that. I wasn't in touch with what my values or passions were anymore; my identity had become subsumed by work. What I decided was I needed time to find who I really was. This is when I left my dream job and chose a different path."

"I found myself searching for meaning in my mid-20s. I had one too many dinners alone in the office late at night, poring over Excel spreadsheets. I thought this couldn't be all there was. I wanted to be involved in building something meaningful, something that had a bigger purpose. At the same time, I realised that there was more to life than material success, particularly if it came at the expense of everything else."

Fallacy of Blind Faith

"I enrolled in a Harvard extension school program while also taking on a demanding new job. It is a heavy workload. However, it has been an amazing outlet for me. It has brought me together with diverse people from across the world interested in renewable energy and sustainability. Perhaps because of the COVID limitations, schoolwork has filled an important gap for me. One where I can get inspired by different perspectives and points of view. I think this is a good example of continuingly challenging yourself and, in the process, feeling energised."

Nightmare of Lost Purpose

"I've seen some high-pressure working environments that champion survival of the fittest. These experiences led to some perverse outcomes and warped judgments. This came to a head when I developed a serious health condition and decided nevertheless to go to the office that day rather than the doctor. I had convinced myself that work was more important than anything else, including my well-being. After I was finally persuaded by someone to go to the hospital, I spent a long time in the waiting room reflecting on which decisions had led me to this point. It was the first time I started questioning whether I had my priorities in order and accepting that my current path wasn't sustainable or right for me."

#

Fabian Clark, Co-Founder Quarter, Entrepreneur, Accountant, and Marketing Guru.

Fabian Clark, along with his co-founder Rohan Radha Krishnan, founded Quarter as a lower alcohol alternative to the high ABV spirits that were the only option. Developing a gin that has just 12% ABV – significantly less than the minimum 37.5% ABV of other gins – they launched the brand in 2021 and are going from strength to strength.

Failure to Launch

"I didn't find launching difficult. There was a glide path from university to internships and graduate programs. What I found more difficult was finding a good equilibrium between making money and feeling like I was contributing something useful. Some of the big corporate jobs are just very soulless. But I think I had to try them to discover it wasn't for me. I think it was an iterative process of trial and error. The restlessness, I think, in this sense, is useful. Keep looking for what's next and whether there is something better."

Gilded Cage

"A great question to ask yourself is, what would you do if you had endless money? It's fascinating to hear people's answers because, often, they are not that exotic. They tend to be simple things that they truly love but don't make them enough money to pay the bills. My advice is, where you can combine what you love with what you choose as a profession, but failing that, make it the reason you do what you do…to enjoy what you love."

The fallacy of Blind Faith

"I recently decided I needed to understand TikTok better, so I hired someone to help me. I think the deeper question is how I knew I needed to understand TikTok. Would someone else in my circumstances not have bothered? My main answer is that as a business owner, you have an innate sense of what is needed for your business to flourish. There is a measure of anxiety, paranoia even that comes with this territory. I see this as a positive stress. A useful thing."

Nightmare of Lost Purpose

"Without question, you need to make a conscious and continuous commitment to tread down a moral road. I believe in this completely. However, another question is, what if you are trying to innovate, challenge, or change existing accepted norms? How far can you go? In some ways, we can see the question of being moral as a defensive and personal question. But what responsibility do we have to try to change existing norms? In advertising, for example, how far can you challenge social boundaries? In my view, if you do so for virtuous reasons, to break down barriers to inclusion or tackle injustice, you should be courageous."

#

Felix Henderson – Co-Founder LookAfter Group, Entrepreneur, Brand Advisor, and Public Speaker

Felix started his career as a journalist before moving into brand consultancy, where he worked with BMW, Samsung, Microsoft, and Gareth Bale, among other clients. He spent four years running his own business in the technology space, building it into one of the most recognisable student brands in the UK. At the start of the pandemic, Felix co-founded 'LookAfter Group', a digital marketing and brand agency that helps future-facing and highly disruptive businesses to grow. Their client base ranges from household brands to global multinational corporations.

Failure to Launch

"I didn't find launching a problem. What I found more difficult was re-starting after an initial knockback. Getting back up again and taking another chance was more daunting the second time around. Ultimately what made a difference for me was asking for help. Once I did, I gradually regained my confidence. I now feel much stronger, more resilient! I now know I can navigate setbacks."

Gilded Cage

"I think you can get carried away and start to believe some of your own publicity. I think it's easy to fall in love with an over-romanticised version of what you are doing. I think it's natural to want to tell people you are doing well. Left unchecked, this becomes a big obstacle when you need to course correct. Therefore, it's really important to stay constantly grounded. Think about it like your power socket, and the earth wire is there for an important purpose. Without it, things can burn down!"

Fallacy of Blind Faith

"I joke with my friends that we will all be replaced by robots in the next 20 years. I think among my contemporaries, we have grown up with this fatalistic view. If you combine this with the greater social isolation imposed by our COVID world, there is a real problem with maintaining relevance and being equipped to re-invent. My biggest inspirations come from meeting new people and being introduced to new ideas. I think ideas are the real future currency. Making an effort to provoke and change your thinking is a top priority for me."

Nightmare of Lost Purpose

"I have three main pieces of advice: (1) Try never to make a big decision in the heat of the moment. Buy yourself time to reflect and force yourself to look at it from at least two or three different perspectives, (2) don't make a decision because you are scared there is no soft landing. You should always try to make an objectively correct decision. In my experience, alternatives tend to emerge after, not before, you decide something significant. And (3) Give someone permission to call you out. You must have someone in your life who you are 100% honest with, no gloss, no exaggeration, no spin, and outside any vested interests."

#

Jack Oswald – Founder and CEO of Cancha and Former Professional Tennis Player

Founder and CEO of Cancha, a unique startup brand making premium sports and travel bags for modern athletes. Jack started Cancha based on his experiences travelling and competing on the international professional tennis circuit. Cancha was born out of the belief that everyone deserves to pursue their passions and see more of the world.

Failure to Launch

"Living life to please others, to meet others' expectations, leads to an enormous amount of pressure and fear. It was only when I recognised this tendency to want to please, to want to make others happy, that I was able to break free and finally find something that was mine."

"It's good to have huge expectations, an ambitious goal. But if all you do is dream of something big, you will achieve nothing. You have to eat the elephant one toe at a time. Achieving a dream ultimately must be translated to a simple first step."

Gilded Cage

"Recognise it is easy to become consumed by the mundane. It's like quicksand or gravity. It's a constant force. You have to remind yourself why you are doing what you're doing. We do have to make some sacrifices to achieve our goals, but I guarantee you there is still beauty along the journey. Make sure you take time to admire it."

The Fallacy of Blind Faith

"I think a strong conviction or purpose can be evergreen. What changes are the tools and tactics to achieve that purpose? If you view your profession as a tool, you may be in trouble. If you view your profession as a conviction, I think you will adapt and re-invent much more naturally."

Nightmare of Lost Purpose

"I do think the world makes us think we have to look good, sound good, and project artificial images of ourselves. There is pressure to be good in small moments. The reality is I would choose to surround myself with people of consistent character and substance. If you allow yourself to be consumed by the superficial, you will likely struggle with leading a moral life. It is better to be yourself, for all the good and bad of that. In my view, authenticity wins in the long run."

#

Yvonne Rieser – Attorney at Law and Entrepreneur

Dr Yvonne Rieser is an Austrian lawyer and Colombian attorney. She is a founding partner of the law firm BBR Rieser Alvarez Abogados, based in Bogota, with an office in Santa Marta and President of Chirimoya Colombia.

Since July 2017, she has been the attorney of confidence of the Austrian Embassy in Colombia and director and board member of the Austrian cultural foundation in Colombia. Before moving to Bogota in July 2015, she worked as an Associate at the Vienna office of the international law firm DLA Piper, in the EU Department of the Austrian Ministry of the Interior and at the International Law Office of the Austrian Ministry of Foreign Affairs. In 2012, she passed with distinction the service examination for civil servants of the General Administrative Service A1/v1 in legal service. She has represented Austria in various EU Council working groups and was head of the Austrian delegation of the Council

140

working group DAPIX (Data Protection and Exchange of Information) in Brussels.

She holds a PhD in law with honours.

Failure to Launch

"I was blessed with great parents who really nurtured and guided me through school, university, and my first law job. It didn't feel difficult for me to transition from student to employee. However, I think while I wouldn't change a thing about how my late teens and early 20s unfolded, in retrospect, I probably trusted the institutional career path possibly too much, simply because I didn't know there was an alternative."

Gilded Cage

"I found myself in my mid 20's at the top of a mountain in Colombia having a conversation with a complete stranger about how we were both very unhappy in our jobs. At that moment, I re-evaluated the path I was on and started to genuinely challenge whether the traditional career path was the only way. It was a seminal moment in my life. Up until then, I think I was following a path of expectations and routine. I quit my job a few months later and decided I would build a life around what made me happy."

"Reinvention for me felt like it was a result of a pivotal moment. A point where I had reason to question whether there was an alternative to the conventional path I was on. Each time I have done that, things have worked out for the better. I love my life today, and I got here because I made those choices. However, it can be really scary to choose between the certainties of a well-paid job versus something less tangible. My advice will always be, don't suffer an unfulfilling existence for lack of an alternative. Trust me, it is there waiting for you."

The fallacy of Blind Faith

"I was on a highly sought-after assessment program waiting for the senior officer's feedback. I realised, as I waited that the very people I was aspiring to join were miserable. They were deeply unhappy with what they were doing. It struck me I didn't want to be like them. In a few weeks, I went from being focused on promotions to changing jobs and industries."

Nightmare of Lost Purpose

"I have taken the view that money and a job are not good reasons to compromise my principles. Fortunately, it has only really happened to me once, but when I saw behaviour I thought unacceptable, I just walked away. It is important that you don't make earning a salary a factor in what you think is acceptable. I understand compromise, but there are problems if you persuade yourself that financial concerns are a good reason to compromise."

#

Ben Towers – Happl CEO, Entrepreneur, Investor, Advisor, and Speaker

Ben Towers is one of 'the most influential entrepreneurs on the planet.' Whilst still only 24 years old, Ben started in business aged 11 and has since successfully exited his marketing agency, invested in disruptive start-ups, and inspired millions. Ben is now on a mission to change health outcomes.

Failure to Launch

"I believe we underestimate opportunities. We impose artificial constraints and limit our thinking. I am amazed at the number of opportunities available if you really put your mind to it. Internships, for example. If you really want to try something, they are a great option."

"Mentors and role models are essential. They can help you visualise a future that might otherwise be elusive. Seek out interesting and inspiring people. You can learn more from a short conversation than reading endless books."

"I agree with the phrase that *the perfect can be the enemy of the good*. It's not a cliché in my view. It is very good advice. Take a practical step over an academic debate any day.
Whether you fail or succeed, you are far better off than if you had never tried."

Gilded Cage

"There is confusion between passion/purpose and profession. Sometimes, they are the same, and sometimes they are very different. Knowing where your energy, your very identity comes from is essential if you want to be happy. I knew what I wanted to do from very early in life. But for others, they need to work at finding it. You'll never find something you don't try to look for."

"I don't underestimate the challenge of financial security. It is an essential building block for achieving your dreams. This is where it is important to be a multitasker. Do what you must while building what you love."

The fallacy of Blind Faith

"Don't get lost in theory. It can be seductive to believe that reading leads to expertise, excellence, and success. In my experience, you are better at trying, experimenting, and iterating. Learn as you go. Get expertise when you need it. Action should be a priority over research."

Nightmare of Lost Purpose

"Achieving clarity of thought is not easy in an increasingly intrusive world. You have to work hard to achieve tranquillity. Know yourself well enough to know how and where you can clear your mind and clear the clutter. Perhaps then you'll be able to see what you're missing."

"I do my best thinking when I completely disconnected. No computer, no phone. Just me, a notepad, sitting somewhere remote, where it's not easy for distractions to interfere."

Authors' Notes

We tend to have 'what do you think you'd say if this happened?' type conversations quite regularly. In the summer of 2022, we were discussing what we'd say if we were asked to give a commencement speech. We argued a little about the utility of commencement speakers. One of us was adamant that it was just entertainment, a means to lighten the ceremony and tell a few jokes. Something akin to an after-dinner speaker. The other was adamant that while that may be true of some commencement speeches, it was possible to share some genuine advice that might help at least one person in the audience.

We then had a lot of fun discussing what that might be. How would each of us attempt to share something with an audience of people who were about to embark on their professional lives? Given the nature of our professional lives, and perhaps because we were enjoying an excellent meal, this morphed into us discussing what we thought were the big 'existential' crises that we had either navigated personally or tried to help colleagues overcome. This book emerged from that discussion.

We hope you enjoy it and at least one reader finds it useful.

Acknowledgments

To the extent, you have enjoyed this book, that is in no small part due to the efforts of the following people. If you disliked it, well, sorry about that. Just remember two things: (1) sometimes doing something you don't like is still good for you, and (2) the people we acknowledge here are certainly not to blame.

Our book is inspired by our study and career experiences. As such, without question, we are standing on the shoulders of others. We have a great many people to thank in this regard, including our various University teachers, mentors, business colleagues, friends, and family. We hope we have done a good job of taking the lessons they shared with us and re-presenting them to a new audience.

Special thanks to Andy Baker for his amazing illustrations and to Rachel Moulton for her early encouragement when Shey was still stuck in his dorm room. Honourable mention to Jim McNeish for his early insights on the psychology of managing career crises.

To our extraordinarily talented next-generation collaborators, without which the second part of this book would have been so much poorer. Izzy Holder & Tony Adams, Noel Ifeanyi Alumona, Emily Buckley, Fabian Clark, Felix Henderson, Jack Oswald, Yvonne Rieser, and Ben Towers. Our discussions and your stories were incredibly compelling. We were so inspired by hearing about your journeys we chose to include summaries of your thoughts so all readers could share the wisdom. We have included short biographies that hint at your combined brilliance. Thank you for taking the leap of faith to collaborate and trust us with your stories. We are certain that more accolades will follow you all in the decades to come.

A special dedication from Dr Schuster to his 95-year-old mother, Elfriede Schuster. There are so many things to thank her for it may take a separate book. I am most grateful for providing me with a good dose of humility and a moral compass that served me so well all my life. Secondly, my thanks to AFS Intercultural Programmes for allowing me to study in the US in my mid-teens. It showed me a global, diverse, very different world and set a foundation for everything I subsequently went on to achieve. Thank you, Daniel Obst, for being such a great President and role model for the NextGen.

A special dedication from Dr Oxley to Sue. Like so many of the best things we have achieved, we did this together. Thanks for all the brainstorming sessions, love, support, encouragement, and coffee. To Charlotte, Amy, Liz, and Rebecca for their love, support and sharing of eccentric English humour. And a very special thanks to Fynn and Lane for giving me a better excuse to be silly and tell Grandad jokes. And finally, to Terry and, posthumously, Shirley, for starting me down this road. I'm not sure quite how I got here, but I know it began in Hither Green.

Reflection Questions

For some people, reading is a solitary pursuit. In an increasingly intrusive world, finding quiet moments to hide away with a good book seems like a great way to tune out and relax. Depending on what you choose, it can be meditative and inspiring. It may be tempting to think of this as a lonely pastime, but that has not been our experience. When you are immersed in a book, you are in a dialogue with the words, the story, your imagination, and the connections that serendipitously occur.

For others, reading can be very social. Book clubs are popular. But beyond those, we seem to be in an era where sharing has proliferated. If you see or hear something noteworthy, you share it with others. Part of this is just fun, almost gossipy, and part of this is genuine enthusiasm to share something interesting with a friend. Indeed, we reference the value of being able to discuss problems or challenges with trusted friends or colleagues. We think gaining others' perspectives is like looking through different windows and seeing slightly different angles of the same object.

When we finished our manuscript, we discussed whether we wanted to include some discussion questions at the end. Some books do this in anticipation of encouraging book club sponsorship. Our conclusion was that we only wanted to include something helpful, thought-provoking, or fun that amplified the contents of the book. If you want to search classic book club questions like 'What was your favourite part of the book' or 'who was your favourite character', by all means, go ahead.

What we have done instead is come up with three short lists for reflection. These are designed in the spirit of the foundational purpose of our writing collaboration: (1) Relevant and pragmatic, (2) entertaining, and (3) humorous. We have written these for both solitary and social readers. Questions that don't require broader discussion but that could be fascinating to discuss with others.

Relevant and Pragmatic

1. Do you think you might have or are currently experiencing one of the career crises caricatured in the *A Career Carol* fable? If so, have you tried the 'career hacks' suggested in Part 2 of the book?

2. If you haven't yet experienced the crises we discuss in this book, do you think you will be able to avoid them completely? Is it better to avoid these crises if you can or demonstrate your resilience by navigating through them?

3. Is it better to critically examine where you are and whether you are genuinely happy or to soldier on and not ask too many awkward questions?

4. Have you always known what you wanted to do with your life or has it evolved and changed over time?

5. Do you live to work or work to live? Is work a necessary evil to allow you to do what you love, or is work central to what gives you fulfilment?

Entertaining

1. Is there any significance in the names of each of the characters in the fable?
2. Do you agree with Shey's views on commencement speakers? What is your reasoning?
3. Make a list of people in your life that might be proxies for the ghosts in the fable.
4. What do you think Shey saw at the end of the commencement ceremony?
5. Of the quotes from the NextGen leaders interviewed, list your top 5. Why did you pick them?

Fun

1. Can you feed two people at the Olive Garden for under $15 (breadsticks are not a valid answer)?
2. The sunscreen reference in the opening chapter is from what commencement speech? Was that speech ever actually given at a commencement ceremony?
3. If the four ghosts who visited Shey were real-life celebrities, who would they be?
4. What is Shey's passion? If you applied the lenses, we suggest in Part 2, what would you guess is Shey's true passion?
5. Suggest a musical soundtrack artist for each chapter in the fable.

If you would like to share your answers to these questions with us and the broader *A Career Carol* community, you can tag us at:

Website:
www.DrsSchusterandOxley.com
LinkedIn:
https://www.linkedin.com/company/drs-schuster-oxley
Twitter:
https://twitter.com/DrSchusterOxley
Instagram:
https://instagram.com/a_career_carol?igshid=YmMyMTA2M2Y=
YouTube:
https://www.youtube.com/channel/UCE2bhfvi3A19Cd76MSXLCuA
TikTok:
https://www.tiktok.com/@drsschusterandoxley?is_from_webapp=1&sender_device=pc